ROBERT RAY KING

JULIA NÁNAY is a descendant of Transylvanian ancestors. She came to the United States subsequent to the Hungarian uprising of 1956. Miss Nánay graduated Magna Cum Laude, Phi Beta Kappa from UCLA in 1973 with a degree in political science. She has received two Master's degrees from the Fletcher School of Law and Diplomacy (Tufts University) in international economics and energy studies, 1974 and 1975 respectively and is presently working for Northeast Petroleum Industries in Boston, Massachusetts.

PROBLEMS BEHIND THE IRON CURTAIN SERIES NO. 10

TRANSYLVANIA:
THE HUNGARIAN MINORITY
IN RUMANIA

by

JULIA NÁNAY

Library of Congress Catalogue Card No. 76-19730

ISBN 0-87934-015-0

C 1976 Danubian Press, Inc. Astor, Florida, 320002. U.S.A.

Printed by: Bethlen Press, Inc.

FOREWORD

In the course of my graduate studies at The Fletcher School of Law and Diplomacy, I became interested in the question of minorities. Having been born in Budapest, Hungary of parents who are of Transylvanian extraction, I was raised with an awareness of the problems encountered by a number of groups on the periphery of what is present day Hungary. I quickly came to realize that concern for these groups was more than just a passive exercise in futility. It was a very real part of the Hungarian consciousness. The attempt by surrounding states to assimilate these minorities has served to fire already burning sentiments of nationalism.

The concept of minorities in the United States is a very complex matter politically, historically, traditionally, economically, legally, as well as emotionally. Many nations live together in the U.S.; nations whose race, language, history, traditions and religions differ. The U.S. is alone in the world in basing its population growth on multinational immigration. Therefore, its minority problems cannot be compared with those of any other area.

I have tried to present the minority question in Transylvania as a mirror in which you can see and measure the use and abuse of plain politics in dealing with groups who were not immigrants to the land that serves as their home but, in fact, the first settlers and original inhabitants of this land.

This study may be considered as a small and modest portion of a much larger picture depicting how politicians handle the minority problem in Europe, particularly in Eastern Europe. I am very thankful to my professor, Uri Ra'anan, for his early comments and to Dr. Albert Wass and Dr. Paul Csonka without whose help and encouragement this work could not have been completed.

TABLE OF CONTENTS

TABLE OF CONTENTS

The omnipotent Communist Party and the Hungarian minority.

A framework of internationalism. Marxist-Leninist methodology for the treatment of minorities. Different perceptions of the concept of fatherland.

A "Greater Socialist Rumania" as a slogan for national unity in Transylvania. Stalin's cultural manipulations.

The ethnic composition of Transylvania.

The Rumanian census.

Forced population exchanges between Transylvanian and Rumanian cities. The alteration of the composition of urban populations.

An investigation into the suppression of Hungarians in Transylvania by the U.S. Congress. The report of the International Commission of Jurists.

The Groza Declaration. The intervention of the International Court of Justice.

The Hungarian Autonomous Region, the Hungarian People's Council and the de-Magyarization actions.

The Hungarian Revolution in 1956. Its influence on Rumania. The alarming situation in Transylvania.

A Danubian Federation. *The New York Times* examines the explosive situation in Transylvania.

Gheorghiu-Dej, Stoica and Kádár meet. Sentencing Hungarians in Transylvania after the Hungarian Revolution. Cultural, economic, educational sanctions after the revolution. The merger of the Hungarian language Bolyai University with the Rumanian Babes University.

Cultural socialization. Districts redrawn and population exchange further reinforced.

TABLE OF CONTENTS

page

New Soviet policy as regards Hungarian minorities in Rumania and in other annexed territories.

Abolishing the 16 regions in Transylvania and establishing 40 counties and 2,706 communes. A breakdown of Hungarian communities.

Rumanian statistics omit categorizing minorities.

Rumania denounces the Soviet invasion of Czechoslovakia. Gestures toward Peking and Yugoslavia. Soviet fears of a possible Balkan coalition. Solutions to the problem of minorities in Transylvania.

Showing population of nationalities in larger cities.

Nationalism has a thousand faces.
It blurs the vision of the man with
the sharpest eye. It invades every
human weakness. It deals in tradition, piety, pride in race, professional jealousy, in all virtues and
vices.   —Ady Endre

INTRODUCTION

Faced by the challenges of a rapidly changing world order, the eighteenth century unleashed a number of revolutionary forces which today continue to play a vital role in Eastern European politics. None, however, has lent itself to as much controversy and emotional reverie as the force generated by nationalism. Receiving its impetus from the French Revolution, it is perhaps the single most important factor governing relations within the Soviet bloc. Nationalism has emerged as one of the heroic stalwarts of national unity and, oftentimes, of minority anguish.

Growing out of a mythical conception of an ideal fatherland, Eastern European nationalism is based on a set of deeply-rooted socio-political beliefs wherein each country has developed its own special brand of collective pride. This collective pride is an "emotional fusion and exaggeration of nationality and patriotism."[1] To be sure, nationalism received its impetus from the French Revolution, but it did not commence with the French Revolution. This latter is a purely arbitrary and perhaps fallacious assumption made by many writers on the subject. Nationalism, as a sense of cultural identity, existed prior to 1789. However, it was not until the revolution, with its accompanying proposition that individuals and communities have a right to attach themselves to whichever states they wish, that nationalism acquired territorial and political connotations. Properly stated, the French Revolution provided the climate of thought from which the doctrine of nationalism could finally emerge in the early nineteenth century.[2]

The concept of nationalism is a European invention which assumes different shades of meaning in the Eastern sector than in the West.[3] It purports to supply a theoretical construct for the principle of sovereignty advanced by the French Revolution. The construct remains theoretical because no doctrine can provide

11

concrete criterion whereby nations may be isolated from one another owing to the complexity of the modern nation-state system. According to the Declaration of the Rights of Man and the Citizen: "The principle of sovereignty resides essentially in the Nation." The problem arises when one attempts to define what exactly constitutes the nation, how it is related to the state, and what role is assigned to the government and the individual in the nation and the state. Sovereignty naturally introduces a whole new gamut of propositions which, in one way or another, attempt to deal with the Kantian formulation of the free will as it is embodied in the right of a people to national self-determination. Undoubtedly, we could devote this whole essay to defining nationalism but due to limitations of time and space, we will deal only briefly with the arguments it presents.

A nation, in the tradition of the French Revolution, refers to a group of individuals who exercise their will collectively in the choice of a particular form of government. Carlton Hayes derives his definition from the French tradition, positing a nation to be the citizens of a sovereign state. Taking note of these details, we can draft a more precise design of the nationalistic scheme. We can say that a nation is a number of individuals who, in pursuit of self-determination, will themselves to be its members.4 The autonomous will or the free will of the citizens is expressed in the state, which derives its legitimacy from the nation. National determination becomes the determination of this autonomous will while nationalism is the doctrine which provides the criterion for the right determination of the will.5

In the multinational framework of modern nation-states, it is difficult to recognize the nation-state as anything other than an ideal form of political organization. Ideally, as Schleiermacher ascertains, the best political arrangement arises when each nation forms a state on its own.6 The absence of any model examples of such arrangements in the twentieth century necessitates speaking in purely abstract conceptual terms. The state must assume the responsibility of preserving the unity of the nation, thus integrating the political with the cultural and emotional life of the masses.7

Within this theoretical construct, therefore, the state functions to maintain order in the nation and becomes a sort of guiding body, simultaneously directing and being directed by the nation. This paradoxical allocation of roles leads to a distinction between the political nationality and the personal nationality of a nation. The two are as much independent as they are interdependent. In its organized form, political nationality manifests itself in the state apparatus which administers the day-to-day affairs of the nation. Personal nationality, on the other hand, is tied to various considerations of language, religion, race, customs, and traditions which determine the peculiar identity of the nation.8 Political nationality involves loyalty to one's state; personal nationality, to one's nation. Both are distinguished from patriotism which involves loyalty to one's fatherland (terra patrie) or its institutions. There is a sense of love for one's country which enters into patriotism. This affection factor naturally plays a part in the individual's identification with a specific nation, but it is not incorporated in the doctrinal make-up of nationalism.

Finally, by making the state commensurate with the nation, by submerging the personal component under the political component of nationality, one is confronted with the problem of national minorities. So long as the state tolerates the personal-political distinction and restricts its activities solely to the political sphere serving equally the interests of all nations under its jurisdiction, this problem does not in fact arise. A minority becomes a national minority only when its interests diverge from those of the state.9

In the fervency of its appeal, Eastern European nationalism directs a keen eye to this question of national minorities. Nationalism only sharpens tensions among different groups in mixed areas. Since it desires a redrawing of boundaries and a revamping of the political machinery to meet the demands of a particular nationality, it tends to upset whatever order has been achieved in the society, to resurrect settled disputes, and to further polarize the diverse national groupings. Any expression of nationalism brings to surface the problem of national minorities which, in the Eastern European case, is particularly acute. Governmental efforts to suppress the mere existence of the issue have only magnified its significance and aggravated the forces seeking a resolution. For despite innumerable attempts to administer healing solutions, the wounds inflicted by centuries of violent struggle have not been remedied by repeated applications of Western medication.

13

Historical Transylvania is much smaller than the area known today by that name. Transylvania now refers to the entire area acquired by Rumania in 1920, including a wide strip of the Hungarian Plain (Crisana and Maramures) and a portion of the Bánát.

14

The complexity of the problem of national minorities in Eastern Europe renders any discussion of the overall picture impossible within the scope and limits of this paper. My intention here is not to confuse but to clarify; not to lecture but to analyze. This is not a study on nationalism per se, nor is it a detailed treatment of the minority question in the Soviet bloc. On the contrary, it is a work restricted in the focus of its inquiries and strictly confined to a specific region.

The area annexed by Rumania after World War I is comparatively small, 103,903 square kilometers (40,700 square miles) to be exact, but the tensions generated by this annexation are immense.10 Size then is not indicative of importance. For more than fifty years now, Transylvania has been a hotbed of nationalistic fervor unparalleled by any in Eastern Europe, and the cause of constant friction between Hungary and Rumania. The main point of contention is the treatment by Rumania of Transylvania's minorities. This author feels, moreover, that the Transylvanian minority problem deserves considerably more attention than it has received in the past. Our primary concern here will be to illustrate its broad significance through the plight of the Hungarians confined to that territory.

This study, then, restricts its inquiries to a specific area and a specific group. Its message, however, extends far beyond the mere geographical entity it purports to examine. It would like the reader to consider the plight of countless millions trapped in such minority groups. Relegated to the position of second class citizens, they are embroiled in a struggle to uphold their cultural identity in states which are dedicated to destroying it. Transylvania is just one example of a compact unit locked in this frustrating struggle. It undoubtedly remains one of the steaming cauldrons of nationalistic sentiment in the European community where the reconciliation of Magyar interests with those of the state has been rendered virtually impossible. Thus, without any further hesitation, let us direct our attention to the Transylvanian question as a case study in Eastern European nationalism.

Nationality does not aim either at liberty or prosperity, both of which it sacrifices to the imperative necessity of making the nation the mould and measure of the State. Its course will be marked by material as well as moral ruin, in order that a new invention may prevail over the works of God and the interests of mankind.

—Lord Acton

II.

THE BIRTH OF THE NATIONAL MINORITY QUESTION
IN TRANSYLVANIA

History can boast of few injustices as glaring as the decisions made at Trianon. While the treaty makers of 1919 assigned one-fifth of the population of East Central Europe to nations to which these people did not want to belong, the measures forced upon Hungary were perhaps the harshest of all. On the principle of the people's right to self-determination, the thousand year old Hungarian Kingdom was shorn of nearly three-quarters of its area and two-thirds of its inhabitants.11 With the dismemberment at Trianon, territories and peoples formerly Hungarian were distributed among seven different states: Austria, Czechoslovakia, Poland, Rumania, Yugoslavia, and Italy, with Hungary left holding a very small remainder. While to the south, the Serbians took Croatia and Slavonia as well as a portion of the Bánát of Temesvár, Rumania received the rest of the Bánát to the southeast, as well as a part of the Hungarian Plain and the much disputed territory of Transylvania.12 In effect, Rumania acquired an area greater than that left to the sadly truncated Hungarian nation. Consequently, 1,704,851 Magyars became subjects of the Kingdom of Greater Rumania.

What occurred at Trianon in June 1920 was only one of many fruitless efforts to resolve an issue which goes far beyond the question of a mere border dispute. Regarding the world in terms of "spheres of influence," the victorious powers committed a grave historical blunder. They ignored the ethnic map of the Danubian Basin and with a series of dictatorial measures, passed off the

16

problems of smaller nations as unimportant.13 In short, the Paris Peace Conference did not light the liberty torch for East Central Europe. It set flame to an already burning Hungarian national consciousness which considered the Treaty of Trianon a humiliating form of degradation and refused for one moment to accept its "terms of shame." The slogan itself became one of "Tria-Non," "No, No Never!" and the question of minorities and frontiers became a national obsession.14

The obsession had its roots in considerations that long preceded Trianon. Nationalism was a deeply embedded phenomenon in Eastern Europe, one that had acquired increasing significance before the victors met to pass out judgment. It was by no means a sudden wave of national passion that gripped the region in the interwar years but a protracted form of group allegiance. Before considering the aftermath of the peace settlement, it would be wise to examine Rumanian and Hungarian claims to Transylvania from a geographical and historical perspective. Not only will this prove helpful in furthering our understanding of the complexity of the national minority problem, but it will serve to clarify existing antagonisms in the area. Transylvania, after all, is one of the "problem children" of Eastern European nationalism.15

Transylvania's strategic importance derives from a multifaceted appeal. Geographically, the region is an integral part of Central Europe; politically, it functions within Eastern Europe; culturally, it is very much attached to Western Europe; historically, it is an amalgamation of all three of these factors. Poised on the far eastern edge of Europe, her position was unparalleled in the defense of Western civilization from the Byzantine threat. Open towards the west, the southwest and the south, the province is enclosed from the northeast, southeast, and the south by the Carpathian Mountains and the Transylvanian Alps. These mountains present a barrier some six hundred miles long, reaching altitudes of over 7,000 feet. There are few passes through the range and no wide roads leading into Rumania proper.16 Consequently, the geographic division of Transylvania from the Regat (Rumania Proper) is almost complete, posing not only major problems of communication but also helping to preserve the area's Hungarian character. For while Transylvania is practically cut off from her administrative organ on the southeast, she is geographically linked

17

to her neighbor on the northwest. This vital link with Hungary extends beyond mere natural unity. It provides a sort of spiritual force which keeps the flame of Magyar nationalism burning and, in a sense, sharpens the xenophobic factor in Transylvanian-Rumanian relations.17

From the time of its formation in 896 A.D., down through the Middle Ages and modern history until 1918, Transylvania did in fact constitute an indivisible natural, political, and economic unit with the Hungarian Kingdom.18 This historical antecedent is precisely the grounds for Hungary's claim to Transylvania. Rumania's argument is one of Daco-Roman continuity which asserts pre-Magyar ties to the area.19

It is interesting to note that prior to the end of the thirteenth century, three "ruling nations" existed side by side in Transylvania: the Magyars, the Saxons, and the Székelys.20 The exclusion of the Wallachians, who were essentially the early Rumanian settlers of the region, from this triumvirate is probably a major cause of minority tension in Transylvania even today. Their further exclusion from the "Union of Three Nations" in the fifteenth century and from the Constitution of 1542 sharpened their resentment against the Magyars.21 In view of the fact, however, that the victims of the anti-Habsburg and anti-Turkish struggles were predominately Magyars and Székelys, by the close of the eighteenth century, the Wallachians formed the real majority in Transylvania. Whether the Rumanians were in Transylvania prior to the Hungarians is a subject of constant dispute. The fact remains, however, that before the eighteenth century, they neither acquired the numbers nor the status which could give them equal recognition. The changing world order ushered in with the 1700's began the era of Rumanian national consciousness.

Having set the scenario for this unabated conflict, suffice it to say that the eighteenth century only sharpened existing frictions. After the turbulent years which followed Turkish and Habsburg domination in Hungary, the twentieth century did not bring with it any measure of relief. World War I brought added strife, and the order it endorsed saw a renewal of chaos.

Basing their title to Transylvania on Daco-Roman continuity, the Rumanians laid their cards before the victorious Powers at

18

Trianon. Clemenceau drew first, and the others followed. A strong Little Entente on Germany's eastern flank was highly desirable from Clemenceau's perspective. Rumanian claims were sealed with approval and another boundary casually disrupted. Hungarian nationalism thereafter directed all its spiritual energies towards resurrecting the pre-War greatness of the Hungarian Kingdom. This strong revisionist tendency in the Hungarian political outlook was reflected in domestic and foreign policy, blurring any efforts to normalize relations with the successor states. The Treaty of Trianon reinforced the uncompromisingly conservative character of the Magyar nation, laying the groundwork for its fascist future.22

Hugh Seton-Watson diagnosed the Transylvanian situation as follows:23

Transylvania . . . cannot be considered as a Rumanian province with a Hungarian minority or as a Hungarian province with a Rumanian minority. It is the home of both Rumanians and Hungarians, both of whom have lived there far longer than any historical records that can be considered reliable. Until the two nations can live together in peace and friendship, it is inconceivable that the country can have any prosperity or security.

Prosperity undoubtedly envisioned an independent Transylvania or at least one which was loosely linked to both Hungary and Rumania for security purposes. While the simultaneous federalization of Transylvania with Rumania and Hungary was unlikely after World War I, prospects for a Kossuth type of Danubian Federation were also discarded.24

Equality, unfortunately, is never desirable to those who hold positions of power. It was certainly unattractive to the Rumanians who savored the opportunity of dealing out repressive measures against their Transylvanian minorities.25 In the aftermath of Trianon, the campaign to subdue minority strength involved an extensive drive for "Rumanianization" more intense than any ever undertaken by Hungary.26 Countless measures were devised to dissociate the tightly knit Hungarian community.27 The Rumanians implemented a complete social revolution along national lines, displacing the Hungarian, German, and Jewish bourgeoisie. For while Rumanians formed the national proletariat prior to World War I,

19

with the acquisition of this rich territory, they intended to carry out a campaign of forced cooptation at the expense of groups which previously constituted the elite.28 The alienation of Hungarians, Jews and, although to a lesser degree, Germans from the new system forced these groups to unite in the face of possible annihilation.29

Rumanian land reform expropriated 2,718,146 acres of land belonging to Hungarians.30 Primarily the holdings of small landowners, the properties were handed over to the Rumanian churches and people. The Orthodox Church was the principal beneficiary of these measures. Reform deprived the Lutheran, Protestant, and Catholic Churches of much of their lands. These losses constituted the greater part of their wealth.31

Parochial education was also dealt a heavy blow. In light of the general impoverishment of the churches under land reform and oppressive taxation, denominational education was left to witness its own demise.32 Schools where Magyar was retained as the language of instruction were faced with considerable hardships. According to available data in 1931, the ratio of students to Rumanian language institutions of elementary school age was ninety-three per school whereas lack of adequate facilities to accommodate Hungarian children brought that ratio to three hundred sixty-five per school. The elementary school population ratio was one institution to 766 Rumanians and one institution to 1187 Hungarians.33 Many children were thus forced to seek an education in institutions using the Rumanian language. In a survey of forty-nine towns in Transylvania where the proportion of Hungarians was 63% and where there were 68,000 children of school age in the year 1932-33, only 16,000 children or 24% were able to attend the Hungarian denominational schools. The state had limited enrollment to that figure.34 Oftentimes, moreover, the state refused to recognize minority schools as public institutions. Certificates issued by these schools were considered inferior to the ones issued by state-run Rumanian schools.

The inequities inherent in the "Rumanianization" of the educational process spilled over into other areas as well. By various methods of juggling data, conducting population exchanges among cities, gerrymandering district lines for political representation, Rumania was able to insure the existence of an indigenous urban majority in once predominantly Hungarian districts. The following

20

statistics released in 1930 indicate the population shifts resulting from forced "Rumanianization:"35

Nationality	1910		1930	
Total	776,262	100.0%	963,418	100.0%
Rumanian	151,800	19.6%	338,000	35.3%
Hungarian	480,000	62.0%	368,000	38.4%
German	123,000	15.9%	127,000	13.3%
Others	19,000	2.5%	123,000	13.0%

Since government in Eastern Europe is the chief employer of labor and the main source of income for the citizens, the exclusion of minorities from its ranks can be a cruel form of injustice with devastating effects. Many Magyar speaking employees were barred from their jobs to make room for the Rumanian population. Language examinations were imposed on those remaining so as to find an excuse for their elimination as well. Statistical data for 1933 estimates the following breakdown in government employment:36

Type of Employment	Total	Rumanian		Hungarian		Others	
County Administration	1,109	789	71.2%	209	18.8%	111	10.0%
District Administration	839	513	61.2%	142	16.9%	184	21.9%
District Notary	1,602	949	59.2%	344	21.5%	309	19.3%
Municipal Administration	1,532	901	58.8%	357	23.3%	274	17.9%
Municipal Notary	139	119	85.6%	11	7.9%	9	6.5%
State Supreme Court Judges	78	73	93.6%	4	5.1%	1	1.3%
Employees of State Court	153	130	84.9%	20	13.1%	3	2.0%
Superior and Municipal Judges	691	576	83.3%	65	9.4%	50	7.3%
Superior and Municipal Employees	2,926	2,193	74.9%	529	18.1%	204	7.0%
Superior Court Attorneys	62	59	95.2%	1	1.6%	2	3.2%
Attorneys' Assistants	78	62	79.5%	14	17.9%	2	2.6%
District Court Attorneys	13	13	100.0%	—	—	—	—
Attorneys' Employees	15	12	80.0%	3	20.0%	—	—
Total	9,237	6,389	69.2%	1,699	18.4%	1,149	12.4%

While Rumanians were given as the largest numerical element of the population, they were also the most backward. All the cities awarded to Rumania were founded by Hungarians or Germans. The cultural, ethnic and civic life of the region is, therefore, almost exclusively a product of their energies. Turkish vassalage had left its toll on Rumanian civilization. Their approach to the treatment of minorities reflects the bitterness of former servility.37 Underlying the Rumanian population shifts in the inter-war period was a desire to accelerate development. The strong Rumanian presence in county, district, and municipal jobs in 1933 is indicative of a conscious effort to suppress the Hungarian minority.

Intelligently construed, the national idea should never lead to oppression. In Rumania, where the boundaries of the national government could not be made to coincide with those of each nationality, where diversity was abundant and homogeneity almost non-existent, where the will of the majority constantly felt threatened by that of the minority, the national idea led to divisiveness, persecution, and resentment.

Hungary was unable to reconcile herself to the loss of her Transylvanian territories. Still nursing her wounds when World War II approached, she was being drawn closer to the folds of Magyar revisionism while attempting to resist fascism. Invariably, however, fascist Italy and Nazi Germany loomed in the foreground as the bastions of salvation against the Bolshevik threat and further Little Entente intrusion.

1940 was a decisive year for both Hungary and Rumania. In June, Rumania was forced to cede Bessarabia and northern Bukovina to the Soviet Union. In August, Bulgaria received southern Dobrudja. Hungary too began pressing her claims for Transylvania. Perturbed by the frontier disputes and the revisionist tendencies of Eastern Europe, Germany and Italy decided to resolve the issue of Transylvania by partition. The Vienna Diktat gave northern Transylvania to Hungary and left the southern portion to Rumania. Rumanian census figures reported that the population of the area reannexed to Hungary was composed of 1,007,170 Hungarians; 1,166,434 Rumanians; 60,046 Germans; and 160,234 Others (mostly Hungarian speaking with non-Hungarian names). The portion

The 1940 Vienna Diktat returned northern Transylvania to Hungary while leaving the southern portion for Rumania.

23

still attached to the Regat had 473,551 Hungarians; 2,067,723 Rumanians; 481,128 Germans; and 133,000 Others.38

This irresponsible carving up of territory generated disastrous consequences for both Rumania and Hungary. The partition created havoc where it should have restored order, exaggerated anomalies where it should have mitigated tensions. The boundaries imposed on Transylvania by the Axis dictators cut the region in half, inviting economic chaos and a renewal of ethnic strife. The line was drawn with complete disregard to geographical, administrative, and ethnic factors. There was a frantic scurry to transfer goods and people from one area to the other. The Rumanian Government immediately ordered all movable goods from the North to be brought to the South and introduced repressive measures against Magyars remaining in their territory.39

While the complications arising from this division were immense for the two parties involved, the problem was momentarily resolved for the Germans. Transylvania was their whip to force their allies into submission, one day promising the prize to Hungary and the next, offering it to Rumania.

Thus, as World War II took its course, Germany was bolstered by two allies who were hopelessly opposed to each other, not particularly united behind Hitler, but commonly hostile toward the Soviet Union. Combating its primary enemy, Judeo-communism, Rumanian nationalism envisaged a Greater Rumania for Rumanians. Encouraged by the reincorporation of northern Transylvania, Hungarian nationalism sought to recapture Hungary's former eminence. Although both were goaded on by the German Führer's promises, Hungary still cringed from involvment in the war. Not even visions of a greater Hungarian Kingdom could muster all-out support for the German effort. But what future hopes could not accomplish, circumstance was able to resolve. When Hitler's soldiers marched across the Hungarian frontier, all thoughts of recourse to neutrality were momentarily lost behind the gloomy shades of war. The extraordinary sequence of events in 1941 left Hungary no alternative but to cooperate. The Axis bonds were solidified with the Hungarian nation participating as an unwilling German satellite.

Rumania, on the other hand, supported Germany from the start. However, as the fighting progressed, her position became somewhat more ambiguous. German losses at Stalingrad in 1942 made Bucharest reconsider the alliance that had been formed. Hitler's defeat could be a serious blow to her expansionary aspirations. When, therefore, the Red Army reached the mouth of the Danube River, deep within the frontiers of Rumania, panic and demoralization took hold of the populace. On August 23, 1944 Rumania suddenly switched camps and thrust the Soviet troops into the Carpathian Basin.

Triumphant in the Soviet victory, Rumania anticipated her share of the spoils, casting a hopeful glance toward Transylvania. In order to placate Bucharest for Soviet annexation of Bessarabia and northern Bukovina, Stalin annulled the 1940 Vienna Diktat. It was thus that northern Transylvania was reannexed to Rumania and the latter witnessed the restoration of her 1938 boundaries.

When the issue of Transylvania actually came up for discussion at the Peace Conference in May of 1946, the United States favored Hungarian retention of a northwestern strip of Transylvania including Satu Mare and Oradea. The Hungarian aide mémoire asked that Hungary receive a region which included those towns as well as the towns of Nagy Károly, Nagy Bánya and Arad, but no participant ever bothered to read this mémoire. When the American Secretary of State, James F. Byrnes, advanced the proposition that in his de facto annexation of Transylvania Mr. Stalin should perhaps consider Hungarian demands, Mr. Molotov replied that the entire province had to be awarded to Rumania because "Mr. Stalin had so decreed."40 The U. S. ultimately was not opposed to Mr. Stalin's decree. Foreign Minister Georges Bidault of France was absent. Those present conceded to Mr. Stalin's decree and the area was ceded.

The New York Times, in an article by C. L. Sulzberger, referred to the award as the "greatest political plum of any Rumanian Government" since the Treaty of Trianon.41 One year and two months later, Mr. Sulzberger wrote:"While admittedly Transylvania is one of those areas whose perfect future is impossible to find, the manner in which its disposition was settled was just another indication that at times this peace is being made on strictly power politics lines."42 For Hungary, the Peace Treaty of February 10, 1947 seemed to be nothing more than a reflection of Trianon, and the anxieties of the interwar period were transformed into silent bitter resentment.

☆ ☆

> How little worthy of respect is the man who roams about hither and tither without the anchor of national ideal and love of fatherland; how dull is the friendship that rests merely upon personal similarities in disposition and tendencies, and not upon the feeling of a greater common unity for whose sake one can offer up one's life; how the greatest source of pride is lost by the woman that cannot feel that she also bore children for her fatherland and brought them up for it, that her house and all the petty things that fill up most of her time belong to a greater whole and take their place in the union of her people!
>
> —Friedrich Schleiermacher

III.

THE SOVIET APPROACH TO MINORITY PROBLEMS

Postwar Eastern Europe stepped into a new phase of development in which the model was not only provided by the Soviet Union but rigidly enforced by it as well. A revolutionary process was underway to remold societal, political, and economic conditions with special attention to the prescribed Soviet image. Socialist transformation demanded a complete reappraisal of the Western value system and a renunciation of traditional patterns of behavior. It required a reassessment of what constitutes a Marxist outlook on nationalism.

Underlying the tangled catalogue of Eastern European grievances was a network of intra-bloc hostilities. The Transylvanian question was far from reaching any substantive conclusion, and the fate of the Hungarian minorities was yet to be determined. Delineating Eastern Europe as a Soviet "sphere of influence" certainly left unresolved the issues plaguing national minorities. Their position after the war was even more precarious in terms of loyalties than it had been prior to Russian subjugation.

27

Translyvania was confronted with a curious web of allegiances. There was, of course, the omnipresent Communist party with its leading body, the Soviet Union. There was also Rumania and the party branch it would foster. Finally, there were the innate attachments to the fatherland of its various sundry nationalities. The most perplexing task of all was integrating these allegiances into a Marxian framework of proletarian internationalism.

In the process of achieving homogeneity, Marxism had to contend with a variety of contradictory themes: unity and diversity; tradition and modernity; continuity and change; consensus and conflict; political socialization and social fragmentation. It was constantly trying to reconcile differences between goals and achievements, theory and practice, ideals and realities. With the acquisition of Eastern Europe, the most serious confrontation of all occurred. Since Marx had failed to provide any working methodology for the treatment of minorities, the Soviets were hard pressed to reconcile Western nationalism with Communist internationalism. Because their approach to the Transylvanian question was dictated by a Marxist interpretation of the nationalistic syndrome, let us examine the context in which they viewed the problem.

Carlton Hayes defines "nationality" as a "group of people who speak either the same language or closely related dialects, who cherish a common historical tradition, and who constitute a distinct cultural society in which, among other factors, religion and politics have played important though not necessarily continuous roles."[43] The combination of these factors conditions the individual's loyalties. Allegiance to one's nation-state is placed above all other loyalties in this scheme, presuming of course that this is the nation-state arising out of a "corporate will." A belief in the messianic role of this entity is central to the individual's thinking. Patriotism is associated with a love of the fatherland and the sacredness of the Patrie. Since patriotism and nationality both evoke a high degree of sentimentalism, it is only natural that they should be fused in a common frame of reference designated by nationalism.[44]

We have to approach Marxism with this theoretical construct in mind. In his treatment of the national question, V. I. Lenin observed, "Marxism cannot be reconciled with nationalism, be it even of the most just, purest, most refined and civilized brand. In place of all forms of nationalism, Marxism advances internationalism, the amalgamation of all nations in the higher unity..."45 Nationalism, for Lenin, was strictly associated with capitalism and imperialism. Theoretically, the unity of the proletariat transgressed national boundaries and rejected any selfish love of the fatherland. But, in practice, the Soviet Union became the supreme and sacred fatherland where the leadership was to be buttressed by the complete and total allegiance of the masses.

The attitude of the Bolshevik leaders toward nationalism was in line with the traditional Marxist interpretation which cast shades of economics over every reformable facet of society. They recognized immediately that the people's right to self-determination could be exercised progressively or retrogressively, depending on the guidance provided by the Soviet Union. The more backward a people were in their economic development, the more they would be reliant on the Soviet Socialist Republic. Nationalism was highly progressive as a movement in the colonial and semi-colonial world where the nation was still attempting to ward off the binding chains of capitalism. But once nationalism entered the stage of capitalism, its dependence on the Soviet Union was greatly weakened and in presenting obstacles to socialist transformation, it became retrogressive and undesirable.46 If it was to survive in Eastern Europe, Communist internationalism obviously required the suppression of nationalism. Only its suppression could resolve the contradiction between consensus and conflict, theory and practice. Despite the grim facade of harmony and socialist cooperation which prevails today, the nationality problem continues to gnaw at the sides of the satellite regimes.

The Transylvanian situation after World War II was characterized by conflict and disunity. Conflict was a key factor owing to the geographical and historical conditions we have described earlier. Disunity was a direct consequence of a meshing of allegiances. Transylvania's integration into an internationalist Marxist framework was theoretically feasible, but the abolition of centuries of national conflict by indoctrination was practically impossible.

Stalin advanced cautiously at first, making friendly overtures in all directions. He was shrewd enough to realize that a rigid and dogmatic approach to ethnic problems would invariably result in mass alienation. Identification demanded a gradual reconciliation of existing contradictions, a slow process of synthesizing ideals and

29

realities. He, therefore, introduced the Stalinist National Policy which recognized ethnic autonomies in Transylvania and urged their federated coalescence. The slogan now being "A Greater Socialist Rumania," these autonomies were to be "nationalistic in form, socialistic in substance."47 This substance was derived from directives issued in Moscow and implemented through Bucharest.

In December 1948, the Politburo of the Central Committee of the Rumanian Workers' Party advanced a resolution on the national question.48 It repeated the Stalinist adherence to "equality in diversity among nationalities liberated from the class yoke." The resolution also referred to Stalin's speech of April 6, 1948 at the signing of the Soviet-Finnish treaty of friendship in which he spoke of equal sovereignties. Finally, it commended the Rumanian Workers' Party on its efforts to halt the persecution of minorities and promote friendly ties between Rumanians and other nationalities living in the new Rumania. Hinting at the spread of anti-Sovietism, the document acknowledged the need for its suppression.49

Rumanianization thus gave way to Bolshevization. The various aspects of the "nationality" argument were utilized so as to effectively Bolshevize the diverse cultural units in Transylvania. Language, skillfully manipulated, became a vehicle for the dissemination of propaganda. The party created a rapport with the population by communicating with each group in its own language. Party supervision insured the tightening of dependency on the Soviet Union politically, economically, and culturally. Strict surveillance of the communications media also insured ideological dependency.

The Soviet Union recognized the importance of ideology in maintaining cohesion and as a means of legitimizing political power. In light of the Leninist conviction that human consciousness can be manipulated politically, it was necessary to saturate the population with every bit of information considered relevant to the party's ideology. The object was to influence national consciousness, and the role of the media in developing the national identity was not to be underestimated. Propagating the notion that the workers have no fatherland, the media was able to transform Marxist doctrine into a vehicle of nationalism. The Soviet Union became highly adept at reorienting its satellite states toward a new form of control in which socialist identity, political ideology, and organization were more important than parochialism, the family, and regional loyalty.

Rational is perhaps not the best description one could accord a totalitarian regime, but in its attempt to institutionalize revolution by pulverizing the existing associations in society, the communist regime acts with a great deal of rationality.50 Stalin appropriately began with the recognition that the social composition of Transylvania was rooted in diversity and characterized largely by overlapping associations. Compromise was necessary to solidify the communist stronghold. Once the regime was firmly entrenched, alternate courses of action would be available.

The ethnic composition of Transylvania (including Maramures, Crisana, and the Bánát) in 1930 was returned according to race as 57.9 percent Rumanian, 24.4 percent Hungarian, 9.8 percent German, and 3.2 percent Jewish.51 The population breakdown for Rumania as a whole in 1930 was 72 percent Rumanian, 8 percent Hungarian, 4 percent German, and 4 percent Jewish. Ruthenians, Russians, Bulgarians, Turks, and Gypsies were also listed. While in Rumania as a whole Hungarians were distinctly outnumbered by the indigenous population, their numerical force in Transylvania was significant.

The revised statistics for 1952 indicate the population distribution for Rumania as a whole, but the criterion being used is that of mother tongue (language spoken best or most readily). The 1930 census emphasized race. The mother tongue--race distinction was evidently made to accommodate the inflated statistics which included many Jews and "Others" under Rumanian census figures. The distinction is purely arbitrary and a matter of semantics because, in fact, it is difficult to delineate the linguistic from the racial criterion of nationality.52

The mother tongue categories of 1952 were 85.7 percent Rumanian, 9.4 percent Hungarian, 2.2 percent German, and 1.8 percent "Others." Comparing these with the 1930 figures for Rumania as a whole, there is a 13.7 percent increase in the Rumanian population, only 1.4 percent in the Hungarian, a 1.8 percent decrease in the German, a 3.1 percent decrease in the Jewish (in 1952 they constituted 0.9 percent), and a phenomenal 12 percent decrease in

"Others." The exact population distribution according to nationalities (mother tongue being the criterion employed) for Rumania as a whole in 1952 was as follows:53

Rumanian	13,597,613	85.7%
Hungarian	1,499,851	9.4%
German	343,913	2.2%
Yiddish	138,795	0.9%
Gypsy	53,425	0.3%
Serbo-Croatian	45,447	0.3%
Russian	39,332	0.2%
Ukrainian	37,582	0.2%
Czech-Slovak	35,143	0.2%
Turk-Tatar	28,782	0.2%
Bulgarian	13,408	0.1%
Greek	8,696	0.1%
Armenian	6,987	0.0%
Polish	6,753	0.0%
Albanian	735	0.0%
Others	15,639	0.1%
Not declared	523	0.0%
Total	**15,872,624**	**100%**

The decrease in Germans after 1945 can be accounted for by postwar Kremlin policies designed to eliminate the "German menace." While the Rumanian Government did not expel the German population, it inflicted harsh measures against them. Though many had fled with the retreating German Army, massive deportations to Siberia helped to deplete their remaining numbers. The minority was actually reduced to half its size. The reduction in figures for the Jewish minority is due in part to Nazi atrocities and in part to the postwar inclusion of Jews in the Rumanian category.

Any critical observer of Rumanian census figures learns to detect the inconsistencies. It is clear from the available data that the Rumanians are intent on broadening the majority-minority gap. There is, moreover, a fine line to be drawn distinguishing race and language and an even finer line distinguishing language and nationality. Most attempts to define nationality have incorporated the language criterion. It is pivotal to the scheme Hayes devises. Schlegel and Fichte place undue emphasis on the linguistic component while C. A. Macartney specifically identifies nationality with language. The delineation of the two can best be interpreted by Hans Kohn's formula postulating a "corporate will." Reminiscent of the general will argument advanced by Rousseau, it is useful in perceiving the fine distinction actually made by the Rumanians. However, for all practical purposes, in terms of gathering census data, the validity of drawing this line can be questioned. By choosing to categorize minority groups according to language, Rumanian census officials were able to bypass the malaise inherent in the "corporate will." Individuals were not required to choose national alignments, but only to assert which language they spoke most readily. Many in the 1952 census were reticent to reply directly, preferring to be listed as Rumanian-speaking. In 1956 the race and mother tongue criteria of former years were replaced by the sharper language-nationality distinction. Individuals were then asked to identify not only their language, but their desire to belong to a specific nationality as well. They were called upon to clarify their "will" to belong, that is, to choose between the majority or the minority. The choice was not an easy one. The obligation to state before officials one's national priorities was enough to drive a wedge between a people and its culture and served superbly as an instrument for intimidation. Pressure on the Hungarians to "denationalize" themselves became intense and unremitting.

The nationality and language figures for 1956 were as follows:54

	Nationality	Language
Rumanian	15,011,190	15,086,923
Hungarian	1,589,443	1,651,953
German	382,400	391,388
Yiddish	144,198	34,263

The data was revised in 1960, apparently to account for some discrepancies in the earlier figures:

	Nationality	Language
Rumanian	14,996,114	15,080,686
Hungarian	1,587,675	1,653,700
German	384,708	395,374
Yiddish	146,264	34,337

There is a decrease in the Rumanian sector in the revised table both in terms of language and nationality, with an increase in Germans and Jews. The Hungarian figures stay much the same but still favor language after the revision. For every 1,000 people of declared Hungarian origin, there were 1,042 giving Hungarian as their mother tongue. Although it is somewhat bewildering to think that Hungarian would be the language of persons who were not of Hungarian origin, 4.2% of the Hungarian minority preferred not to admit to their Magyar origins.

While the 1956 and 1960 figures given above apply to Rumania as a whole, they are indicative of conditions in Transylvania. The most useful method for identifying population trends is by examining the available data.55

City	Population			
	1910	1930	1956	1966
Brasov (Brassó, Stalin)	41,056	59,232	123,882	140,500
Cluj (Kolozsvár)	60,808	100,844	154,752	167,930
Oradea (Nagyvárad)	64,169	82,687	99,007	111,657
Tirgu Mures (Marosvásárhely)	25,517	38,517	65,188	77,042
Timisoara (Temesvár)	72,555	91,530	142,251	152,552

The data for Hungarians and Rumanians in these cities is available for 1910 and 1930:

City	Hungarian		Rumanian	
	1910	1930	1910	1930
Brasov	17,831	24,977	11,786	19,398
Cluj	50,704	54,776	7,562	34,836
Oradea	58,421	55,039	3,604	20,914
Tirgu Mures	22,790	25,359	1,717	9,493
Timisoara	28,552	32,513	7,566	24,088

During the interwar years, Rumania realized that something would have to be done to counterbalance the relative strength of the Hungarians in the towns. Population shifts proved useful in diminishing minority proportions. Since Bolshevization in the 1940's did not altogether nullify the Rumanian solution to nationality issues, population shifts to urban areas after World War II continued to be used to reduce Magyar numbers in Transylvania's cities. This is evidenced above by the tremendous increases in Rumanian settlers in Cluj, Oradea, Tirgu Mures and Timisoara. While some of the statistical growth was due to declarations of Rumanian nationality out of fear of reprisal, there was also a sudden influx of Rumanians from the Regat (Old Kingdom) to the major cities. Even as Hungarians were vigorously discriminated against in the issuance of settling permits, Rumanians were encouraged to immigrate. A survey of population shifts between 1910 and 1956 in twenty-five Transylvanian cities serves to illustrate the effects of forced Rumanianization.56

	Hungarian Sovereignty		Rumanian Sovereignty		
	1890	1910	1938	1948	1956
Hungarian	58.3%	65.3%	46.6%	41.0%	36.0%
Rumanian	15.8%	15.6%	32.0%	47.9%	51.9%

The 1956 Rumanian census showed 6,069,535 people in Transylvania and the parts of the Hungarian Kingdom annexed to Rumania in 1920, all of this now being called simply Transylvania. This compares with 5,257,467 in 1910, the date of the last Hungarian census for historical Transylvania. The overall increase over a forty-six year span was less than one million. While part of the increase is natural, some of it is due to the settling of Rumanians from Bessarabia and Rumania proper in Transylvania, especially since German and Jewish war losses in the area were in excess of 600,000.

In 1910 there were 1,661,805 Hungarians in Transylvania. Their number in 1956 decreased to 1,618,246 while Rumanian figures increased from 2,838,454 to 4,192,506. Historical Transylvania, of course, was smaller than today's area but most of the increase is due to a planned program of shifting population.57 Irrespective of approximately 200,000 Hungarians who were forced to leave Transylvania after World War I, no other mass exodus has taken place. The statistics point to a methodological elimination of the Hungarian minority. If the population had been allowed to grow under normal conditions, it would most certainly have reached the two million mark over the given forty-six year span. It is altogether unlikely that the Hungarian minority would have decreased by 43,559 while the Rumanian population increased by 1,354,052.

Since the numerical increase of Rumanians in Cluj (Kolozsvár) is especially striking between the two wars, we should focus closely on post-1945 developments in that city. Cluj is the capital of Transylvania and the largest city ceded to Rumania after Trianon and the annulment of the Second Vienna Award. It is today surpassed only by Bucharest in size.

Year	Total Population	Hungarian	Rumanian	German	Others	Footnotes
1910	60,808	50,704	7,562	1,676	866	58
1930	100,844	54,776	34,836	2,702	8,530	59
1948	117,915	67,977	47,321	360	2,257	60
1956	157,723⁻	74,155	74,033	990	8,545	61

While the growth of Cluj between 1910 and 1930 was the direct result of a threefold process of industrialization, urbanization, and Rumanianization, the increase after 1948 can only be explained by a deliberate attempt to swell the data in favor of the Rumanian majority or by forced population shifts. That is, the urbanization and industrialization which occurred after 1948 were greatly intensified by the drive for Rumanianization. Hungarians were driven from the urban to the rural areas to seek opportunities for employment, scarce as these opportunities may have been. It was no longer a threefold process passed off as a facet of modernization but rather a single campaign to totally assimilate or eliminate the Hungarian minority.

According to the statistics for Cluj, the total population increased by the same proportion in the twenty-year period between 1910 and 1930 as it did in the eight years between 1948 and 1956. Unlikely as this may seem, one is led to surmise that the information is significant but not wholly reliable. The 1948 figures are based on the 1939 census correcting for births and deaths but not for immigration. The increase between 1930 and 1948 was probably larger than these figures indicate. Thus, in the absence of sufficient reliable data on minorities, the detection of discrimination has become a process built on inconclusive evidence.

In the 1947 Paris Peace Treaty, the Hungarian minority was awarded certain rights partly as a result of Stalin's cautious approach to the ethnic problem and partly in appeasement of the American delegation's insistence that Hungary should be permitted to retain the Crisana-Koros region. Despite the treaty's attempt to formulate safeguards for minorities in Rumania, communist terror after 1946 was vigorously exercised against all non-communist segments of the population, especially that of the urban middle class.

In terms of actual protection offered by the Peace Treaty for the minorities, let us examine a number of its provisions and some violations.

The agreement concluded in February 1947 between the Allies and Rumania asserts in Part II, Section 1, Article 3 that:62

(1) Rumania shall take the steps necessary to secure to all persons under Rumanian jurisdiction, without distinction as to race, sex, language, or religion, the enjoyment of human rights and fundamental freedoms, including freedom of expression, press and publication, of religious worship, of political opinion and of public meeting.

(2) Rumania further undertakes that the laws in force in Rumania shall not, either in their content or in their application, discriminate or entail any discrimination between persons of Rumanian nationality on grounds of their race, sex, language or religion, whether in reference to their persons, property, business, professional or financial interests, status, political or civil rights or any other matter.

Much like the Treaty of Versailles, the 1947 agreement clearly contained safeguards to embrace all minorities regardless of ethnic considerations. Language alone was sufficient to bring a group under its protection. The Groza Government underwrote Rumania's guarantees toward her national minorities and pledged its adherence to the principles of "equality, democracy, and justice with respect to the entire population."63

But despite Rumania's guarantee toward her minorities, there were many flagrant violations of human rights which drew an outcry of protest from the West. On April 2, 1949, the United States and Great Britain sharply criticized the Rumanian, Hungarian and Bulgarian governments. Forwarding all three a list of violations of guarantees included in the peace treaties, they ordered them to "stop the inhuman acts which accompanied their political and economic reforms."64 On July 11, 1949, the Soviet government rebuffed the Western powers for interfering. The matter was then referred to the Fourth Session of the General Assembly of the United Nations where it was held in abeyance until the International Court intervened. When told to appoint an arbitration commission to investigate the breach of peace treaties, the governments concerned simply refused to comply. The condemnation of these actions by the General Assembly on November 3, 1950 went unheeded. At one point, the International Court concluded that "the disregard shown by the Rumanian government for the rights and liberties of persons under its jurisdiction...has indeed become so notorious as to evoke the condemnation of free peoples everywhere."65 Without replying to the Court's accusations, the Rumanian government proceeded to formulate a new constitution.

Particularly striking, both in terms of the peace settlement and the Rumanian constitution of 1952, are the provisions designed to safeguard the cultural rights of the minorities. In the constitution anyway, a conscious effort seems to have been made by the Groza Government to meet minority demands. Article 82 permits the use by each group of its own language and provides for the establishment of educational institutions at all levels to teach each group in its mother tongue. Administrative and judicial organs are authorized to use the language of the majority nationality in their respective area. There is also a stipulation for the appointment of civil servants from the majority group in each area. We can see why the Rumanian government organized massive population shifts. While these provisions were supposedly intended to protect the minorities, the official policies enacted by the leadership did everything possible to moderate their effect. The majority nationality in most areas was Rumanian, if not by nature then by force.

The constitution went on to assert that it was the duty of the State to protect the culture of national minorities "which ought to be socialistic in its content and national in its form." This was precisely the idea underlying the process of Bolshevization. It also characterized Stalin's approach to the minority problem. The government was actually permitted to dictate the socialistic content of minority culture. If this content did not agree with what was nationally desirable, the leadership could enforce whatever measures it considered necessary to make the two coincide. It is interesting to note that Article 81 designates "any kind of chauvinistic persecution of non-Rumanian national minorities" as "a criminal offence."66

One of the most striking provisions of the constitution concerned the creation of the Hungarian Autonomous Region (Articles

19, 20, 21), an administrative district that had a 77.3% Hungarian majority (565,510 Hungarians). The other groups were as follows: 20.1% Rumanian (146,830), 0.4% German, 0.4% Yiddish, and 1.5% Gypsy.67 Tirgu Mures (Marosvásárhely) was designated as the capital of the Hungarian Autonomous Region. The 18 regions specified in the 1952 constitution now included this territory, embracing the parts of Transylvania with the greatest concentration of Hungarians.68 The Hungarian political association, the National Democratic Union (MADOSZ), had been urging the creation of such an autonomous region, and it was due in part to their efforts as well as to some insistence from Moscow that the matter was thus concluded. It would not be wrong to presume that the pressure exerted by the International Court also had a role to play in its formation.

The main concentration of Hungarians, other than the strip of territory along the border, is in the eastern part of Transylvania where some 700,000 Székelys reside. This particular stretch of land, lying about one hundred miles east of the frontier, became the focus of Articles 19, 20 and 21. Modeled on the autonomous regions within the Soviet Republics, the Hungarian Autonomous Region embodied the principle of "genuine proletarian internationalism." It was the perfect area for experimentation with a "socialistic national culture." And, since ethnic identity is most intense along the border, this was the perfect area for conflict avoidance. The creation of an autonomous region in the immediate vicinity of the Rumanian-Hungarian frontier would have enlivened an already burgeoning nationalism. As it was, the established region was somewhat removed to the east, satisfying MADOSZ claims and alleviating the tensions Stalin sought to soothe.

The Rumanian government was thus able to meet Hungarian demands. It established an autonomous administrative territory, removed from the border with Hungary and surrounded by regions that were predominantly Rumanian. Contrary to an homogeneous state model which specifies that once a territory gains autonomy along nationality lines, it should be allowed to elect its own representatives at the regional and municipal levels, the Hungarian area functioned under much the same conditions as the other administrative divisions. The "autonomous administration" provision contained in the constitution was realized only in theory, not in practice. Articles 20 and 21 clearly stated that the laws of the Rumanian

People's Republic governed the Magyar area along with the other regions of Rumania. Any statute drafted by the largely Hungarian People's Council had to be ratified by the Grand National Assembly of the Rumanian People's Republic.69

Then, a disruptive factor entered into the slowly stabilizing Rumanian picture. Even as communist officials from Moscow, Bucharest and Budapest flocked to the Magyar Autonomous Region to express awe and approval for the smooth functioning of "proletarian internationalism," the Hungarian Revolution erupted. Stalin's death in 1953 sparked the desire for de-Russification, but the revolt in 1956 stressed the need for further de-Magyarization. The momentary crisis in the communist leadership provoked by Khrushchev's call for de-Stalinization was followed by an explosive reaction on the part of the atomised Hungarian people, a reaction which breathed life into the limp body of Transylvania's minorities.

Revolutions as bloody as the October massacre of 1956 are not often recorded in the annals of history. 25,000 casualties were reported in an ordeal which commenced as a peaceful demonstration by students and ended as a full-scale battle by an entire nation against Soviet occupation. Far from increasing political stability or political liberty in Transylvania, it attested to the fact that nationalism in mixed areas makes for tension and mutual hatred.

The Rumanian government of Georghe Gheorghiu-Dej was alarmed. It confronted the occasion in the great Rumanian tradition of siding with the keeper of the key to power, namely the Soviet Union. During the upheaval in Poland in 1956, both Gheorghiu-Dej and Chivu Stoica, the Premier, had been in Yugoslavia to confer with Tito over the worsening situation in Hungary and its effects on the rest of the communist bloc.70 In Rumania's case, there was rightful cause for panic since any change in Hungary's posture could put pressure on that country for the recasting of Transylvania's frontiers. The disruption of equilibrium and the reopening of the border issue was the last thing Dej wanted to face. Upon hearing that students in Hungary were urging the formation of a Danubian federation, presumably incorporating Transylvania, Gheorghiu-Dej and Stoica cut short their visit to Yugoslavia.71 They hurried back to Bucharest on October 28, 1956. The possible installation of a liberated anti-communist government across the border was enough to trigger immediate Rumanian reprisals.

40

Despite stringent measures directly enforced to calm the revolutionary fever, demonstrations and student outbreaks swept across Transylvania and Rumania proper. On October 27, 1956, demonstrations were reported in Bucharest, Iasi, Cluj, and Timisoara. Rumanians too were eager to shed the armor of Soviet subjugation. The withdrawal of Russian army divisions stationed in their territory since the end of World War II would have been a much welcomed event. But for Gheorghiu-Dej, it was not a desirable prospect. Soviet troops, after all, insured his political survival. His sudden return from Yugoslavia was sparked by a comprehension that armed intervention in Hungary offered the only sure guarantee for keeping his government in power.

The mood was one of sullen defiance in Transylvania where invocation of the Stalinist dictate urging "revolutionary vigilance" increased the momentum of national patriotism. The "No, No, Never!" slogan of earlier days acquired a sharper edge as it cut deep into the fiber of Eastern European communism. Hungarian nationalists in Transylvania affirmed their belief that political and cultural matters were inseparable and that no culture can live if it is not developing freely in a sovereign state exclusively its own.72 The limited autonomy of the Hungarian Autonomous Region offered little in the way of satisfying minority demands. It seemed as if the Peace Treaty of 1947 and the 1952 Constitution were purely illusory settlements of a problem which could find little hope for resolution in the Rumanian system.

The first published Rumanian comment on the 1956 incident was an editorial in *Scinteia* on October 28, 1956 wherein the Rumanian Worker's Party pleaded for minority support. In a series of articles written for *The New York Times*, Welles Hangen, the only Western reporter allowed into Transylvania at the time, unmasked the turbulent developments there. He described the Hungarian Revolution as a situation over which "Rumanian communist forces might not be so sanguine ... as they would like the outside world to believe."73

Both Rumanian and Soviet army units were stationed in the Hungarian Autonomous Region and other parts of Transylvania. Their chief bases were at Timisoara and Arad. When Soviet troops were ordered to Hungary from these bases to help quell the rebellion, reinforcements were quick to arrive in anticipation of resurgent Magyar enmity in the area. Hungary, it was said, was going through "the inevitable process of democratization."74 Hungarian rebels were denounced for their "hooligan acts of plunder and bestial hangings" as well as "acts of vandalism and crimes of unparalleled ferocity."75 Meanwhile, Rumanian communists spoke of "growing friendship among Rumanian and minority nationalities."76

Irrespective of Rumanian claims of friendship, there was only tension and heightened animosity. Army units with sub-machine guns and rifles patrolled the streets of Cluj. On October 29, students in Bucharest were said to have torn up their communist membership cards in open protest. Students in Cluj boycotted classes on Marxism-Leninism. Reports of outbreaks which included workers and farmers reached the capital. Arrests were widespread and frequent. The Rumanian government persisted in trying to minimize the importance of the whole affair but on October 31, a rumor leaked from Budapest that the police were firing on demonstrators in Transylvania.77 Rumania proceeded to bar foreigners from Timisoara, Arad, Oradea, and Baia Mare. Timisoara and Arad were both used as military bases by the Soviet Union; Oradea controlled the rail line to Budapest; Baia Mare was a potential source of trouble because of its large Hungarian population.78

As riots gripped the country, Rumania's communist regime swore allegiance to Soviet opposition to the Hungarian nationalists. Allegiance meant revenge to Gheorghiu-Dej who threatened to "wage open war against any non-communist Hungarian government."79 Foreigners were confined to Bucharest. The Hungarian section of the university at Cluj was closed temporarily. Welles Hangen was expelled on November 4, making information from the area hard to come by. November 4, 1956 was also the day the Russian army dealt the crushing blow to the revolution in Hungary. For Dej, however, relief was nowhere in sight. With the Russian army back in control, the strenuous task of reconstruction lay ahead.

In retrospect, several remarks can be made about the effects of the Hungarian uprising on the Transylvanian situation and on Hungarian-Rumanian relations. Gheorghiu-Dej hastened to aid the Kádár regime in the restoration of order and in the elimination of the menace of dissidents and counterrevolutionary elements. Of particular importance is Rumania's role in Imre Nagy's execution. For all apparent purposes, the removal of the Hungarian leader from the Yugoslav Embassy on November 23, 1956 with "permission" to go to Rumania was no more than a Soviet hoax to cloak his forthcoming execution. In June 1958, Nagy was executed with some of his colleagues after an investigation and a trial which provoked worldwide shock and indignation. The news of the killings was announced simultaneously in Moscow and Budapest. Although it has never been outrightly proven, Bucharest probably cooperated in the executions.

Gheorghiu-Dej and Stoica led two delegations to Hungary in November 1956 and January 1957 with the purpose of persuading Kádár to relinquish any claims to Transylvania and denounce as chauvinists and nationalists with irredentist aims those who participated in the revolution. Kádár met these requests when he visited Rumania in February 1958. In fact, owing to the weakness of his domestic position and to his reliance on Rumania for aid, Kádár could have done little else but renounce the Rumanian territories inhabited by Hungarians. His statement at a mass rally in Bucharest firmly posits his stand:80

> The Hungarian People's Republic has no territorial or any claim against any country. Anyone who makes such a claim is not only an enemy of the neighboring people's democracies which are living in fraternal friendship with us, but is above all a deadly enemy of the Hungarian People's Republic and of the Hungarian working people who have suffered so much under their past rulers.

Noteworthy in this regard is the fact that the Rumanian government extended aid to the Kádár regime almost immediately after its inception, expressing support with a sixty million ruble loan.81 In her earnestness to establish a neighboring communist stronghold, Rumania was willing to go to any extremes. Some reports even suggested that Soviet deportation trains left Hungary through Rumania. It has also been acknowledged that the reorganization of Hungary's security forces was made possible with Rumania's help. The struggle against "bourgeois chauvinism" and "criminal-minded fascism" was thereby fully launched. Just two years after the events in Hungary, Rumania witnessed the withdrawal of the Red Army from her territories.

While the leadership in Rumania was basking in the full glory of their achievements, Transylvania felt the pains of governmental revenge. Several clergymen, Catholic and Protestant, were sentenced to imprisonment or death. Many Hungarians were arrested under the pretext of dissident activity. According to *The New York Times*, preventive arrests approached the 40,000 mark.82 In 1958, fifty-six of the Hungarian minority were tried. Ten were executed while others received long-term prison sentences.83 Edward Crankshaw of *The New York Herald Tribune* reported that prison sentences ranged from ten to twenty-five years. The families of the imprisoned were often deported to other parts of Rumania, particularly to the marshes of the Danube Delta.84 In November 1964, George Bailey of *The Reporter* summarized the campaign of terror and repression which followed the revolt in these words: "Thousands of Hungarians were arrested, perhaps hundreds put to death. In one trial alone in Cluj, thirteen out of the fifty-seven accused were executed. This year some eight thousand political prisoners were released with considerable fanfare by the Rumanian government in a general amnesty. But as far as I could ascertain in my recent travels through Transylvania, not one of the Hungarians arrested during the revolt has yet been released."85 Mr. Bailey's figures are a bit higher than those of *The New York Times*. His article, however, provides an unequalled first-hand look at the Transylvanian situation in 1964. The article was written eight years after the revolution.

The institution to be hit hardest by the Rumanian axe was that of education. It was here that the first serious contradiction became manifest within a culture that was "socialistic in its content and national in its form." Article 82 of the constitution provided for the establishment of educational institutions at all levels to teach each group in its mother tongue. However, in 1959 it was declared that the maintenance of a bilingual university at Cluj (Kolozsvár) was "in opposition to the interests of socialism" and led to "national isolationism in culture and science (which) just like any other manifestation of nationalism, is a poisoned weapon in the hands of the enemies of the people."86 The promotion of a socialistic culture necessitated the suppression of the national culture and required ethnic minorities to learn the Rumanian language.

Until 1958 education in the Hungarian language was available from the primary to the university level. With the instigation of this "socialist" policy in institutional reform, the number of Hungarian primary schools rapidly declined until it was decreed that only the eldest child could be enrolled for study in his mother tongue. This decree, of course, was in direct defiance of the constitution. Higher education also suffered. Undergoing a process of parallelization, it was obviously doomed to die a slow death. With the introduction of parallel sections that taught in the Rumanian language in minority institutions, the strategy was clear. Once the Rumanian section was established in the system, it could easily overtake and replace the whole Hungarian one.

In 1955-1956 there were 1022 four-year basic schools relying solely on the Hungarian language. By 1958-59, there were only 915 such establishments. Schools with parallel sections increased over the same period from 38 to 124. In 1955-1956 there were 493 seven-year basic schools where Hungarian was the language of instruction. In 1958-1959 there were 469. Schools with parallel sections increased from 10 to 77. [87] By the end of 1962, not a single completely separate Hungarian school remained in all of Rumania.[88]

Interestingly enough, Rumanian data for 1952-53 lists five universities in the country, with the Rumanian and Hungarian sections at Cluj being counted separately. This reference to a distinct department at Cluj coincided with the granting of autonomy to the Magyar region in eastern Transylvania. The 1954 statistics refer to four universities.

In 1958 national minorities were being taught in fifteen languages in 3250 schools and at Cluj in Hungarian. In 1962-1963 this figure grew to 3500 schools with the added emphasis "and at the medical faculty of Cluj University in Hungarian."[89] The change in wording is due to the coalescence of the Babes-Bolyai Universities.

The merger of the Hungarian language Bolyai University with the Rumanian Babes University in July 1959 was a serious blow to the Hungarian minority. The famous University at Cluj now acquired the title Babes-Bolyai University of Sciences. Following this forced assimilation, several members of the faculty committed suicide.[90] Dej announced the merger at a conference of the Union of Student Associations in February 1959, possibly upon a directive from Moscow. The rector of Bolyai University, Lajos Takács, denounced "national isolationism." The rector of Babes University remarked that "the line between Rumanians and Hungarians, between Rumanian and Hungarian professors and students, is an anachronism."91 The scheme was unanimously "approved" at a meeting of students and professors on July 3, 1959. With the parallelization and phasing out process, the Hungarian Institute of Medicine and Pharmacy at Tirgu Mures (Marosvásárhely) lost its autonomy.

The French newspaper, *Le Monde*, dealt with the problem of the merger in 1967 in an on-the-spot report by Michel Tatu.92 Although the distribution of classes in terms of language was not specified at the time of the merger, eight years after its occurrence only 30% of the classes were being taught in Hungarian. While there were 40 graduate students who were enrolled in Rumanian language and literature courses in 1960 with 29 enrolled in similar Hungarian courses, by 1965 the ratio fluctuated in favor of Rumanian course enrollment 218 to 39. This demonstrates an increase of 178 students studying Rumanian as compared to only 10 more studying Hungarian. The discrepancy over a five-year period is admittedly enormous. Moreover, the rector, three of the five pro-rectors, seven of the eight deans, and sixty-one per cent of the teaching faculty were Rumanian. Today, proficiency in the Rumanian language is a prerequisite for admittance and all classes are taught in Rumanian, except those on Hungarian language and literature.93

An additional impact of cultural "socialization" was the systematic dispersal of Hungarian college graduates in non-Hungarian provinces. By 1964 it was estimated that the number of Hungarians living outside their own areas was between 35 percent to 50 percent.94 The placement of most university graduates on a nation-wide basis, rather than according to personal preference, served to scatter Hungarian intellectuals throughout the Regat, thereby diminishing their threat as a concentrated force.

A logical outgrowth of the government's desire to minimize minority pressures was the reorganization of the Magyar Autonomous Region along more integrated lines. The plan for territorial adjustments was placed before the National Assembly at the end of December 1960. In March 1961, Article 19 of the Constitution was amended by the deletion of the phrase which referred to the region as being composed of a "compact Hungarian group." One-third of the Magyar Autonomous Region was attached to the overwhelmingly Rumanian province of Brasov. The detached territory included the whole southern part of the former Hungarian Autonomous Region which consisted of two heavily Székely populated districts. In its stead, three districts which contained a large Rumanian majority were annexed to the remaining Magyar territory from the southwest. The province was renamed the Mures-Magyar Autonomous Region, indicating that it was no longer a solely Hungarian controlled district. Recasting these boundaries inflicted serious casualties on the number of Hungarians, reducing the population by approximately 92,000 (15 percent) in the new province. The Rumanian population grew by 120,000 (15 percent), off-balancing the loss of Hungarian strength.95

The reorganization of the Hungarian precincts through the process of gerrymandering district boundaries was just one facet of administrative discrimination. It was well known that the frontier provinces had the highest rate of industrialization in Rumania and, moreover, that these areas supported a large Hungarian contingent. With a stepped up drive to improve production, Transylvania was overrun by great numbers of civil servants, bureaucrats, and workers from the Regat. They swarmed to the border provinces and the newly created Mures-Magyar Autonomous Region. Here, as elsewhere, the formation of a large industrial bureaucracy of predominantly Rumanian composition squeezed out the Hungarian minority, forcing them to seek work in other areas. Countless numbers of unemployed Hungarians migrated to the Regat where they were greeted with further discrimination. *Le Monde* reported that in 1964 there were more than 250,000 Hungarians in Bucharest.96 Many were again deported as forced laborers to the Danube Delta.97 Management officials in the autonomous province, according to 1964 statistics, were 50 percent Rumanian.

In the Mures-Magyar Region as elsewhere in Transylvania, the use of the Hungarian language was prohibited in the courts and in official correspondences. Its use was even regulated on public conveyances and in stores. But when some Transylvanian Hungarians assembled in Hungary in 1963 to discuss these unfair practices, Kádár had them arrested and imprisoned on charges of "incitement to illegal organization."98 In that same year, an appeal was sent to Moscow by a group of clergymen asking that the Soviet Union take Transylvania for itself rather than leave it at the mercy of the "Rumanian axe."99 The signatories of this demand were sentenced to twenty-five year prison terms. It was indeed as Edward Crankshaw put it, "a smuggled cry to the West." But the cry went unheeded and the Hungarian population awoke to the precariousness of its position as a stranger in a strange land.

☆　☆

Pity then our people Lord
Shaken by disaster!
Since a sea of grief engulfs
Save the Magyar, Master!
Fate of old has rent him sore
May it now bring healing!
Bygone sins are all atoned
Even the future sealing.

—Ferenc Kölcsey
"Hymnus"

IV.

NICOLAE CEAUSESCU SLIPS INTO LEADERSHIP

It was in the Soviet Union's best interests to give Rumania a free hand in the treatment of her minorities. There were, after all, 200,000 restless Hungarians in the Carpatho-Ukraine. Annexed to the Soviet Union after World War II, there was as much potential for rebellion there as in any of the outlying areas of Hungary. Therefore, any easing of restraints in Transylvania could give rise to unrest among nationals in that Soviet territory. What is more, since the Hungarians were never considered as completely reliable elements in the socialist bloc anyway, the Kremlin's attitude toward Rumanian policies vis-à-vis its Hungarian minorities was generally one of complacent approval. It was only with Rumania's growing dissidence in the bloc that Transylvania was suddenly perceived as an attractive tool of Soviet efforts to keep its satellites in line.

Among Hungarians, the revolutionary spirit of 1956 gave way to resignation and at least temporary acceptance of defeat. Persecution led to assimilation; discrimination, to complete subjugation and humiliation. Official boundaries remained as the external symbol of minority existence but not of minority allegiance. The state had successfully imposed its control over a once significant nation enclosed within its territorial demarcation. The policies of the state were those of a national government seeking to eject all foreign elements from its system. Conformity was expected; opposition, rarely tolerated. International peace was no closer to being realized than it had been in the Trianon days of "self-determination."

With the death of Gheorghe Gheorghiu-Dej in 1965, Nicolae Ceausescu slipped into the leadership slot and proceeded to rule from the pinnacles of party power. Deviating somewhat from Dej's Stalinist approach to minority issues, Ceausescu continued to condemn nationalism but eased up on the restrictions his predecessor had endorsed. He admitted that Hungarians should be allowed to maintain their national culture and even initiated some measures to help them do so. A joint publication agreement was reached with Hungary whereby some Hungarian literature that had been banned previously could now enter the country, and a number of provisions were underlined for the translation of selected Rumanian texts into the Hungarian language. However, no book concerning Transylvania could appear in Hungary without the prior approval of Rumanian authorities. Censorship was strict and only books with non-political themes were available to the minority.

The significance of these measures was largely illusory. Little was accomplished in terms of actual contact with Hungary. Whether to increase his popularity or just merely to breathe new life into a decaying situation, Ceausescu's actions were well within the boundaries of permitted freedoms for minorities destined for total assimilation. The liberalizing trend was well calculated. The Hungarian films which entered Rumania in a program of planned film exchanges were often dubbed in the Rumanian language and given subtitles in Hungarian. Theatrical companies from Hungary performed in Bucharest but not in Transylvania. Much of the cultural mainstream flowing into Rumania from Hungary was diverted to Bucharest where the Hungarian population was unduly sparse.

Ceausescu could afford to be more "liberal" in his approach. The pace of transformation had been decided by his predecessor, repressive measures had been taken and much of the opposition had been thoroughly suppressed or eliminated. All Ceausescu had to do was sit back and occasionally extend some show of benevolence toward the minorities.

This benevolence, however, did not alleviate the fears which pervaded the lives of the Magyar populace. The *Neue Zuricher Zeitung* clearly stated in December of 1967 that "the presence of the secret police is still strong. Political opponents and troublesome intellectuals are put behind bars without delay."[100] Surveillance was just as rigid as before, and the constant fear of being reported by informants prevented Hungarians from ever publicizing their true feelings. Transylvania today is probably the only place under communist rule where one still finds such echoes of the Stalinist era as fear of contact with foreigners.

1967 was an odd year in terms of national minority policies. Rumania underwent another reorganization of administrative divisions which completely erased the Mures-Magyar Autonomous Region from state maps. The program drafted in October 1967 abolished the sixteen regions which had been in existence since 1957 and provided in their stead 40 counties and 2,706 communes. The reason specifically advanced by Ceausescu for the drastic adjustments was to facilitate economic management.

Old regions were fragmented into several counties. The Mures-Magyar Autonomous Region forfeited its western districts to Mures County. The loss included the former capital at Tirgu Mures. Its eastern flank joined the Székely areas formerly belonging to the Brasov region. These divisions became effective in February 1968 with a few minor alterations. The Székely area was broken down into two counties where there was previously one. Covasna and Harghita, the two counties in question, were practically the smallest in all of Rumania.101 Although both were predominantly Hungarian, the division subdued their influence. With greater party control of local governments and the state apparatus, their political role was negligible.

Despite the fact that the overall ratio of Hungarians to Rumanians increased in the new county divisions, the latter continued to enjoy a comfortable majority. The only exception was perhaps the case of Covasna and Harghita Counties where Hungarians dominated in terms of proportions (88 percent and 79 percent respectively). To reduce the majority in Mures County, Sighisoara district was added to the detached western section of the former autonomous province. The ratio there was changed from 49 percent Hungarian—45 percent Rumanian to 45 percent Hungarian—50 percent Rumanian. This was a typical example of Bucharest's gerrymandering practices.

While the proportional strengthening of Hungarians in the otherwise tiny counties of Covasna and Harghita was another conscious effort on Ceausescu's behalf to calm minority frustrations, it is interesting to note that after 1967-68, Rumanian statistical

51

sources omit the mention of national minorities.102 Prior to that year, the usual assertion was that national minorities were taught in 3,500 schools and at the medical faculty of Cluj in Hungarian. After 1967 mention is made only of the five universities and in 1972 of six, with the founding of an institution at Brasov. This was just another indication of the slow phasing out of minority education. The obvious conclusion one can draw from this reflects on the nature of a strongly multinational state. Ruled strictly by the majority nationality, it seeks to do away with any tensions between the nation and the state. The two, as in Rumania's case, become inseparable and the principle of national self-determination disappears somewhere in their coalescence, to become itself as illusory as any of the liberties granted to the minorities.

Conditions in Transylvania since the administrative revisions went into effect in 1968 have not improved markedly, but because Rumania's policy of national independence requires the full support of the population, the government has had to meet minority demands to a greater extent. The increasingly independent course pursued by Ceausescu in the satellite bloc has, in turn, given rise to Soviet concern over the future of her captive entourage. This concern was evidenced in Hungary's slightly altered attitude toward the Transylvanian minority question. János Kádár in 1966 expressed resentment against what he termed the "imperialist diktat" of the Treaty of Trianon "which dismembered the territory of Hungary."103

When Ceausescu denounced the Soviet invasion of Czechoslovakia in 1968, his position antagonized other members of the satellite bloc, but it was fully backed by the minorities. At the end of October 1968, national front organizations sprang up nationwide to integrate national minorities into the sudden surge of Rumanian nationalist revival.

The Czech incident and Rumania's anti-Soviet pressure bolstered the popularity of the regime and created a somewhat artificial but significant unity of national forces. But Czechoslovakia did not strike the emotional chords of the Hungarian minority in the same way as the uprising in Hungary. Since that fateful week in 1956 twelve years had passed and much of the hope that once characterized the era had vanished in the gloomy haze of captivity. The demonstrations of support for Czechoslovakia were by no means as massive as those generated by the Hungarian revolt. Owing to the somewhat dubious nature of the liberalization strategy employed by the Ceausecu regime or perhaps merely to emotional stagnation, the intensity of minority support was considerably diminished.

Transylvania, however, did benefit from the Czech incident. Improvements were made in book publications, newspapers, radio broadcasts, and television programs. Hungarian culture received further encouragement to develop but was cautioned to do so only within the framework of this new Rumanian nationalist revival. Hungarians were essentially warned to put being Rumanian ahead of being Hungarian.

Meanwhile, the Soviets applied increasing pressure on Rumania, particularly during the summer of 1971. The Polish Government's decision to let Germans emigrate to West Germany raised several queries in Rumanian quarters. Concessions to the German minority could trigger restlessness in the Hungarian camp, advancing demands from Magyars wishing to emigrate to Hungary. Any mass migration was vigorously opposed. Ceausescu reacted to the Polish decision by engaging the minority groups in Rumania in discussions to solidify their support for his party base.

Soviet concern over Rumania was also heightened by Bucharest's orchestrated gestures toward Peking. Mindful of Yugoslavia's more than casual interest in that sphere as well, the Soviets feared a possible Balkan coalition which would pose a direct threat to their strength in East Central Europe.

The Hungarians, meanwhile, continued to badger Rumania with references to the minorities. Bucharest countered Hungarian attacks by asserting that the party had been "able to solve the national question in the spirit of Marxist-Leninist teaching." In a speech delivered to the Party Central Committee, Ceausescu went on to say, "We must fight for national advancement. We observe the rights of the nationalities and work to ensure these rights. We wish to advance together toward communism."104

Tensions mounted as a Budapest paper commended Austria and Italy for their settlement in South Tyrol of the German minority problem.105 The Soviet Union aired a Rumanian language broadcast, emphasizing its central role in Rumania's acquisition of

Transylvania after World War II.106 *Sovietskaya Rossiya* charged Peking with practicing chauvinism toward its minorities in obvious hidden reference to the Transylvanian situation. The article indirectly drew associations between administrative reorganizations in China which reduced minority proportions in various regions and those in Rumania.107 The article was also transmitted over the radio in Rumanian to sharpen the edge of criticism.108

Ideological warfare meant further easing of tensions, the lifting of some educational and cultural restraints for the minorities and the creation of a sort of illusory aura of freedom. In view of its many years of experience with manipulating circumstances to fit the Rumanian mold and with sacrificing everything for personal advancement, the government at Bucharest has held the minorities well in hand.

Still, the national minority question in Transylvania is far from being resolved. Ideally, Transylvania should be granted full autonomy or be permitted to enter into a Kossuth type of Danubian federation where the emphasis is on cooperation as opposed to assimilation. If Rumania, however, insists on guarding her territorial rights, there are more humane ways of insuring peaceful coexistence within her boundaries. Cultural annihilation is not the solution sought by a civilized government.

The homogeneous state model is one possible alternative for reorganization. It would allow each minority to elect its own representative body. Dividing the country into various regions or cantons, the system would be highly reciprocal insisting that representatives of every ethnic group be stationed in each region to insure the protection of their particular minority. Regional and municipal level leaders would be elected by all citizens but there would not be a parliament.

Due to Rumania's ethnic diversity, however, this model may lead to a high degree of ethnic polarization. Because of the large number of national minorities, although their proportions may be small, a more practical solution should be found. The heterogeneous model would join individual members of ethnic groups in autonomous organizations which are recognized as constitutional entities. The nationalities may still be dispersed, but their dispersal and linkage by such organizations would not introduce the same degree of ethnic polarization as the homogeneous model. Regional, municipal, and central level leaders would be elected by all citizens and there would be a parliament. The regional and central level leaders would oversee the educational functions of all groups.

Of course, the next question one asks is how do these models fit the mold of a communist society bent on practicing proletarian internationalism and preaching the unity of all nationalities. There is no effective parliament in the communist system. There is the party. The candidates for regional, municipal, and central offices are party members. What one has to understand in this case is that no model is perfectly suited for any society. It is only meant for reference and those parts of it which are best suited to each society's needs must be employed. A Hungarian Autonomous Region like the one formed in 1952 could have worked very well had autonomy been granted in practice as well as in theory. The party and the state should oversee the functioning of all such autonomous areas, but they should do so with a desire to facilitate its further existence not to suppress it. For unless Rumania is willing to consider such alternatives of autonomy, there is no way to insure equilibrium. The future holds nothing more than repression, enmity and the further entrenchment of ancient hostilities.

☆ ☆

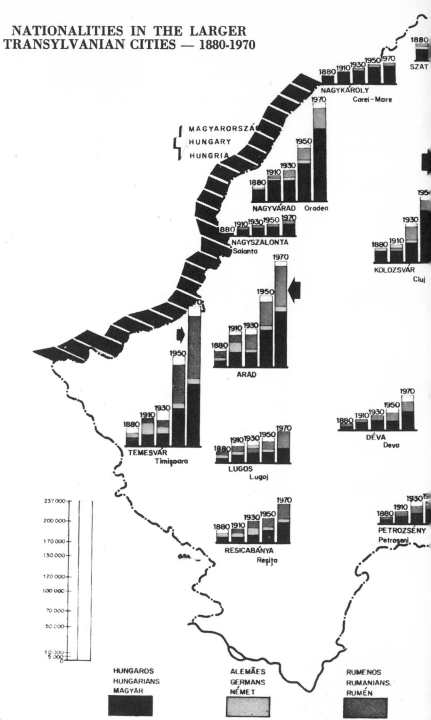

SZAT

NAGYKÁROLY
Carei-Mare

MAGYARORSZÁ
HUNGARY
HUNGRIA

NAGYVÁRAD Oradea

NAGYSZALONTA
Salanta

KOLOZSVÁR
Cluj

ARAD

DÉVA
Deva

TEMESVÁR
Timişoara

LUGOS
Lugoj

PETROZSÉNY
Petroşeni

RESICABÁNYA
Reşiţa

237 000
200 000
170 000
150 000
120 000
100 000
70 000
50 000
10 000
5 000

HUNGAROS	ALEMÃES	RUMENOS
HUNGARIANS	GERMANS	RUMANIANS.
MAGYAR	NÉMET	RUMÉN

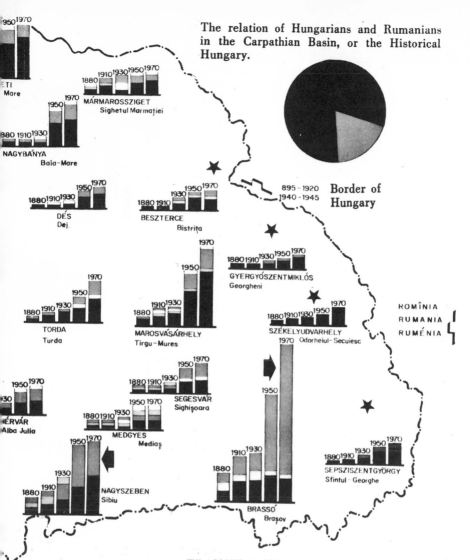

The relation of Hungarians and Rumanians in the Carpathian Basin, or the Historical Hungary.

895 - 1920
1940 - 1945

Border of Hungary

ROMÎNIA
RUMANIA
RUMÉNIA

TRANSYLVANIA
(Part of Hungary during thousand years)

This map represents Transylvania, the south-eastern bastion of the Danube valley. It is separated from Rumania by the mountain range of the Carpathians, heavily timbered and partly covered with snow over a width varying between 50-60 miles. Only four narrow mountain passes ensure the possibility of land communications in the modern sense of the word between Transylvania and Rumania.

Thus Transylvania constitutes within the Carpathian Basin a geographical and historical entity; during the era of Ottoman rule in Central Europe it succeeded in preserving for over a century its identity as an independent Hungarian State.

57

NOTES

1 Carlton J. H. Hayes, *Essays on Nationalism* (New York: The Macmillan Co., 1926), p. 23. The concept of an ideal fatherland is developed in Hans Kohn, *The Idea of Nationalism: A Study in its Origins and Background* (New York: The Macmillan Co., 1961), p. 330. Kohn asserts that "nationalists in Central and Eastern Europe created often, out of the myths of the past and the dreams of the future, an ideal fatherland, closely linked with the past, devoid of any immediate connection with the present, and expected to become sometime a political reality."

2 An excellent treatment of nationalism can be found in Elie Kedourie, *Nationalism* (New York: Frederick A. Praeger, 1960).

3 Nationalism in an Eastern European context is delineated from citizenship and relies primarily on cultural considerations. In Western Europe where the synthesis of the nation-state produced a concept of nationalism with territorial connotations, citizenship is the primary factor in national assumptions.

4 Ernest Renan, *Qu'est-ce qu'une nation?* (Paris: Calmann Levy, 1882), p. 27. Renan expresses this idea of the autonomous will or what he terms "le consentiment" as follows: "Une nation est une grande solidarité constituée par le sentiment des sacrifices qu'on a fait et de ceux qu'on est disposé a faire encore. Elle suppose un passé, elle se résume pourtant dans le présent par un fait tangible: le consentiment, le désir clairment exprimé de continuer la vie commune." In other words, the formation of a nation involves sacrifice; the existence of a nation supposes historical continuity; the survival of a nation depends on a willingness to make further sacrifices and a desire clearly expressed in a 'consentiment' to continue living as a distinct unit. Thus, the will of the individual must ultimately determine whether a nation exists or not.

5 Elie Kedourie, *op. cit.*, p. 81. For Hayes' discourse on nationalism, see Carlton J. H. Hayes, *op. cit.*, pp. 5, 6 and 23.

6 This reference to Schleiermacher is taken from Elie Kedourie, *op. cit.*, p. 58.

7 Interestingly enough, until the latter half of the eighteenth century in Europe, the nobility represented the state and, as such, consummated the bond between state and family. Becoming an extended version of the family, the nobility was often referred to as the "nation." Since cooptation into this privileged class depended on individual merit, the concept of the "nation"

came to express a two-tiered system of the rulers on one side and the ruled on the other. That is, those who succeeded in elevating themselves to the leading class and those who were left behind. Theoretically, the situation was reversed with the French Revolution but, in practice, the elite continued to function under the auspices of a bureaucracy which ruled "in the name of the people." In preserving the unity of the nation, the state was developing the national character, the specific national Kultur. It is this Kultur which assured every individual of his right to belong to his own national state. In his *Ideen zur Philosophie der Geschicte* (*Outlines of a Philosophy of the History of Man*) published between 1784 and 1791, Johann Gottfried von Herder considered the nation-state dichotomy. His concept of "Volk" is similar to what we would refer to as "nationality" or a social group delimited by certain objective bonds. Herder postulated a sort of double balance with the nation and the state on one side and nationality (Volk) and liberty on the other. He weighed the two cautiously and in his estimation, the balance fell in favor of a liberty that must correspond not to an ideal state form but to the needs of each nationality. Unfortunately, Herder's Eastern European followers were not imbued with the same humanitarian values. They were fighting not to preserve the freedom of each nationality but to insure the solid union of the state and the nation, even if it meant overlooking some nationalities. The idea was to submerge the autonomous will under the will of the majority, synthesizing the minority with the majority nationality (the Staatsvolk). See Bernard Suphan ed., *Herders Sammtliche Werke*, XXXIII (Berlin: Weidmannsche Buchhandlung, 1877-1913), XVIII, Briefe zur Beforderung der Humanitat, p. 282. Also see Peter F. Sugar and Ivo J. Lederer ed., *Nationalism in Eastern Europe* (Seattle: University of Washington Press, 1969), p. 13.

8 The treaty makers of 1919 considered race, language, and religion as the determining forces of national consciousness. Language is often considered of particular importance to nationality. Carlton Hayes views nationality as "a group of people who speak either the same language or closely related dialects, who cherish common historical tradition, and who constitute a distinct cultural society in which, among other factors, religion and politics have played important though not necessarily continuous roles." The inclusion of dialects in this definition is significant since it raises many difficulties in delimiting nationalities and, therefore, casts doubt on the linguistic criterion. See Hayes, *op. cit.*, p. 5. Also, see C. A. Macartney, *National States and National Minorities* (London: Oxford University Press, 1934), p. 7. Macartney asserts that each language is "a sort of philosophy which expresses the past history, the character, the psychological identity of those accustomed to it. . . . Many nations have practically identified their nationality with their language, regarding as lost to them those who have ceased to speak it." Johann Gottlieb Fichte designated language as the test by which a nation is known to exist. If it was not constituted into a state, he believed it would be subsumed in a foreign state and thereby cease to exist as a separate entity. The political frontiers which separate the linguistically united members of a nation are purely arbitrary and unnatural. See the discussion in Kedourie, *op. cit.*, p. 68. On the other hand, Kohn, *op. cit.*, pp.

13-14, argues that none of these (i.e., race, religion or language) are essential to the existence of a nationality. He also de-emphasizes the importance of territory, political entity, customs, and traditions. The most essential element for the formation of nationalities, Kohn says, is "a living and active corporate will." This is in line with Renan's 'consentiment' and Kedourie's argument for national self-determination.

9 It is instructive to note that the Treaty of Versailles, Articles 86 and 91, spoke only of 'persons belonging to racial, religious, and linguistic minorities' or of 'inhabitants of (a country) who differ from the majority of the population in race, language and religion.' It does not specifically define what constitutes a "national" minority. The reason behind this seeming evasion can, in fact, be attributed to the need for protecting the interests of Eastern European Jews. Defining nationality in terms of race, religion, or language insured that the Jewish minority would be included among those whose rights the treaty was meant to safeguard. The treaty makers sought to provide a built-in mechanism for the protection of all minorities but, in the long run, this mechanism was not prepared to deal effectively with the problems posed by "national" minorities.

10 We must remember that the historical Transylvania we speak of is much smaller than the area known today by that name. The former, lying east of the Bihar Mountains and fortified to the south and east by the Carpathians, was no more than 57,804 square kilometers (23,300 square miles). Transylvania now refers to the entire area awarded Rumania by the 1920 peace settlement including a wide strip of the Hungarian Plain (Crisana and Maramures) and a portion of the Bánát.

11 Hungary was in fact reduced to 32.6% of her pre-War size and 41.6% of her population. See C. A. Macartney, *Hungary and Her Successors: The Treaty of Trianon and its Consequences,* 1919-1937 (London: Oxford University Press, 1937), p. 1. The German area in the west was given to Austria; the north, Slovak and Ruthene, to Czechoslovakia with some small areas in the extreme north going to Poland; the east, to Rumania; the south, to Yugoslavia with Italy receiving Fiume. In figures this meant that from a territory measuring 325,411 square kilometers prior to the War, Hungary lost 232,448 square kilometers to artificially created multinational states. From a population of 20,886,487, approximately 12,271,370 found themselves in these new states. It was the racial diversity of Hungary which led the victorious powers to summon the principle of the people's right to self-determination. A large segment of the population ceded to other areas was not Hungarian. A concept originally attributed to Marx and emanating from the Kantian autonomous will, the right to self-determination is a vital aspect of communist theory. Lenin summarized its essence as follows: "the political separation of these nations from alien national bodies and the formation of an independent national state." V. I. Lenin, "The Right of Nations to Self-Determination," in *Questions of National Policy and Proletarian Internationalism* (Moscow: Progress Publishers, not dated), p. 52. Lenin did not

speak of the formation of multinational states. The self-determination principle with assertions of Daco-Roman continuity was used to justify the detachment of Transylvania from Hungary. The non-Magyars of the area were provided with the opportunity to exercise their right to self-determination, but Transylvania did not become the "independent national state" Lenin had envisioned.

12 As was mentioned earlier, the entire territory is now referred to as Transylvania.

13 The Treaty of Trianon came complete with provisions for the protection of the minorities in Transylvania. These provisions were to be enforced by the League of Nations which, due to the weakness of its organization, could not meet the claims of the minorities. Unanimous consent within the League prior to the taking of any effective action limited the scope of its activity. Supported by the system of the Little Entente, Rumania was in a position to manipulate the powers of the League in its favor and thus postpone indefinitely any measures aimed at safeguarding the rights of the minorities.

14 In Hungarian the phrase is "Nem, Nem, Soha!". The interwar years also produced the Magyar Creed. Authored by Mrs. Elemer Papp-Vary, it goes thus: I believe in one God (Hiszek egy Istenben), I believe in one Fatherland (Hiszek egy Hazában), I believe in one divine eternal Truth (Hiszek egy isteni örök Igazságban), I believe in the resurrection of Hungary (Hiszek Magyarország feltámadásában), Amen. These are words which even today are inculcated into the youth of every generation to keep alive a faith in the "Patrie" and indeed, to hold up a belief in the reunification of Hungary.

The nationalistic sentiment generated by Trianon testified to the fact that the frontiers which are imposed on a territory do not insure peace nor do they subdue passions. The application of the principle of self-determination later clarified in the "corporate will" nationality argument only aggravated existing antagonisms. The resentment in the case of Hungarians in Transylvania was particularly acute in view of the fact that they were now trapped in a nation where, as foreign members, they were destined for assimilation or elimination. Both these alternatives were greeted by a staunch "No, No, Never!"—a stubbornness which was to cause Rumania many worries.

15 This is to coin a phrase from William F. Robinson, *Nationalism: Hungarian Problem Child*. (Munich: Radio Free Europe Research, July 5, 1967).

16 The famous Hungarian geographer and former Prime Minister, Count Paul Teleki, has written a great deal about Transylvania. In an essay entitled "Transylvania's Situation in Hungary and in Europe," he speaks of Transylvania as an "individual entity with respect to both time and place."

Elie Kedourie, *op. cit.*, p. 125, remarks: "For natural frontiers do not exist either in the topographical sense favoured by Danton, nor in the linguistic which Fichte preferred; ironically, these two conceptions of Nature may even conflict as, for instance, in Transylvania, the topographical features of which endow it with perfect natural frontiers, but which is populated by a mixture of Magyars, Rumanians, and others, long at odds with one another. Frontiers are established by power, and maintained by the constant and known readiness to defend them by arms." Rumania's readiness to defend her title to Transylvania during World War II as well as during the Hungarian Revolution of 1956 bears this out. Geographical unity no longer suffices for the maintenance of modern multinational nation-states. Political considerations override all other factors in the international power balance game.

17 Xenophobia, like patriotism, enters into nationalism but is not a part of its doctrinal composition.

18 C. A. Macartney, *Hungary and Her Successors, op. cit.*, p. 254, asserts that the Magyars entered Hungary at the end of the ninth century but did not occupy Transylvania until a century later. Another theory has it that the occupation of Transylvania came before the occupation of Hungary itself. The truth perhaps embodies all these suppositions. Magyar tribes probably crossed the Carpathians at several different points in the ninth century streaming into Hungary and Transylvania at about the same time.

19 On the subject of Daco-Roman continuity, see Zsombor de Szasz, *The Minorities in Rumanian Transylvania* (London: The Richards Press, 1927), p.12. His account relates that in the second century, the Emperor Trajan destroyed the Dacian state he found in Transylvania and founded a Roman colony. But due to the filtering in of migrating peoples from Asia, after one hundred and sixty years, the colony was relinquished to the Gepides, Avars, Vandals, Huns, and Bulgarians. According to the theory of Daco-Roman continuity, Rumanians are the descendants of Emperor Trajan's soldiers and colonists who stayed behind and intermingled with the Dacian inhabitants. Hiding in the mountains for a thousand years, they reappeared in the twelfth century as a people who still spoke the language and practiced the traditions of the Latin colonists. The plausibility of such a theory is open to question but hisorians like R. W. Seton-Watson have rallied to its defense. See Seton-Watson, R. W., *Transylvania: A Key Problem* (Oxford: Classic Press, 1943). A more plausible explanation is given by Louis Elekes, "The Development of the Rumanian People" (*Hungarian Review*, 1941) p. 678. Elekes believes that "the origins of the Rumanians point to many different components. . . . All European nations have experienced a considerable mixture of blood so that in most cases the racial basis is no longer recognizable. This is naturally the case with the Rumanians who lived at one of the most troubled points of the continent and thus were exposed to many and varied foreign influences." Rumanians are thus seen as an ethno-linguistic mixture of certain Romanized elements persisting in

the Balkans. Of further interest here is a discussion of the continuity principle which appeared in a Hungarian translation of the Rumanian periodical, *Előre* (Cluj-Kolozsvár: November, 1973). In it, the author emphasizes Rumania's Daco-Roman heritage which disclaims any union with the Slavs. The continuity movement, described as taking its roots in the eighteenth century, sought deeper ties with Rome. While it did not sever ties with the Byzantine culture, it popularized the notion that Rome represented the way of the past and the future. Founded in 1700, the Uniate Church was supposed to bridge the gap between Roman Catholicism and Greek Orthodoxy. Perhaps more of a political than a religious institution, it represented a Habsburg-Wallachian alliance at the expense of Protestantism in Hungary. With the advent of communism, the Uniate Church was reincorporated into the Orthodox sect in October 1948.

20 The Székelys populated Transylvania prior to the Wallachian migration into the area which probably occurred sometime in the ninth century. The origin of the Székelys is dubious with some historians postulating a Hun tradition and others saying they are descendants of the Avars. These arguments do not carry much weight in terms of which is more correct, since both the Huns and the Avars were Ural-Altaic tribes, speaking the same language with slightly different dialects. Saxon ancestry can be traced to the Moselle region in Germany. The first Saxons migrated to Transylvania sometime in the twelfth century. Undoubtedly, the Wallachian question is the most difficult one. The great Wallachian migration from the Balkans did not begin until the thirteenth century. By that time the Magyars and the Székelys had blended into one group, forming a significant majority in the region. While Rumanian official statistics do not differentiate between the Székelys and the Magyars, Ceausescu has often drawn the distinction in his speeches so as to show the existence of two small minorities instead of one large one.

21 The Wallachians were excluded from the "Union of Three Nations" at Kápolna in 1438. Documentation is available from 1222 on testifying to the presence of Rumanians (Vlachs, Blachii, Wallachians) in the southern Forgaras district under their own chief or kenezs. The Tartar invasions of 1241-42 inflicted devastating wounds on Transylvania culturally, as well as economically and politically. Reconstruction required major concessions on the part of the government. To secure the cooperation of the nobility, the Hungarian kings donated estates to them. To replace the lost manpower, they allowed Rumanians to migrate to the Bihar Mountains and the Maramures. In order to encourage further migration, Wallachians were recognized as a "nation" in the thirteenth century. But since the Rumanian kenezs were mostly Magyarized by the fifteenth century and no autonomous Wallachian region existed to speak of at that time, recognition was not accorded at Kapolna or in the Constitution. Wallachia and Moldavia united in 1859 and became the independent kingdom of Rumania in 1881. This preceded the Paris Peace settlement by a mere half century. It is as the Rumanian statesman Bratianu once said of Rumania in the course of a public lecture: "With us the Middle Ages began when they ended in other countries. . . . We were

outside the civilization of Europe." See Zsombor de Szász, "Rumanian History," *The Hungarian Quarterly*, Autumn 1941, Vol. VII, p. 205.

22 Revisionism in Hungary is discussed in C. A. Macartney, *October Fifteenth: A History of Modern Hungary*, 1929-1945 (Edinburgh: University Press, 1956, 2 vols.), vol. 1, pp. 3-24. See also the compilation of essays dealing with the question of nationalism in Hungary from feudalism to the present: *A Magyar Nacionalizmus Kialakulása és Története/The Formation and History of Hungarian Nationalism/* (Budapest: Kossuth, 1964). In particular, the treatment by Aladár Kis, "Az ellenforradalmi rendszer reviziós kialakulása (1920-1933)", pp. 302-315 and also Magda Adam, "Az ellenforradalmi rendszer reviziós külpolitikájához, (1933-1941)", pp. 356-395. Hungarian revisionism actually became blatantly manifest when Hungary joined the League of Nations and openly pressed her position in the international arena.

24 Lajos Kossuth (1802-1894) was leader of the movement for national independence and governor of Hungary during the 1848-49 war of liberation. He proposed a Danubian Federation to be composed of all the nations in the Carpathian Basin and the northern Balkans. In 1850 he discussed this plan with Count László Teleki referring to the U.S. as a model organization. At the Moscow Conference in October 1943, Mr. Hull, representing the U.S., and Eden of Britain had blueprints for a Danubian federation but Russia refused to consider them. Transylvania in relation to such a federation was similar to Macedonia in relation to the Yugoslav federation. In both areas, cooperation among several states could have insured stability. The demand for this type of federation was echoed again during the 1956 uprising in Hungary.

25 In reference to the national persecutions which occurred in Rumania, anti-Semitic feeling ran about as high as sentiments against the Magyars since the Jews in Transylvania associated themselves with the Hungarian middle classes and most often considered themselves Hungarian. There was little guarantee of civil liberties for these minorities in the decrees issued from Bucharest and discriminatory taxation policies, language regulations, and land reform measures exacerbated the potentially explosive situation.

26 The so-called "Magyarization" drive followed the Compromise of 1867. In essence, "Magyarization" was an attempt at assimilation. Because the middle and upper classes were composed of Magyar speaking people, those members of other nationalities who were coopted to these classes gradually merged their national identities in a process of assimilating with the Hungarian speaking majority. "Magyarization" was not a contrived effort to forcibly eliminate national minorities.

27 The measures devised by the government were harsher in their implementation than in their actual content. Rumanians are known for the

arbitrariness with which their decrees are executed so that the enforcement of any measure is left to the discretion of government officials. This was especially true in the inter-war years. The paper, *Brassoi Lapok* (December 14, 1925), reported an incident where a teacher in the village of Csikjenőfalva, "in his efforts to enforce the new language regulations of the government, handed out such beatings to his pupils that on the first day the parents had to carry home twenty-four badly beaten children from the schoolhouse, who were unable to walk." Incidents such as this were probably sporadic and not daily occurrences. Nevertheless, this particular piece of evidence is indicative of the way "Rumanianization" functioned.

28 While prior to the changing world order of the eighteenth century the nobility was identified with the "Nation," under Rumanian control of Transylvania, the proletariat came to be identified with the "Nation." This was very much in line with the Marxian call that the proletariat "must rise to be the leading class of the nation, must constitute itself as the nation." The proletariat had to assume the role of the socially progressive class which was previously reserved for the nobility (i.e., bourgeoisie). See Karl Marx and Friedrich Engels, *Manifesto of the Communist Party* (New York: International Publishers, 1932), p. 28. For a further discussion on Marx and nationalism refer to George Lichtheim, *Marxism: An Historical and Critical Study* (New York: Praeger Publishers, 1965), pp. 76-89; See also Robert R. King, *Minorities Under Communism: Nationalities as a Source of Tension Among Balkan Communist States.* (Cambridge: Harvard University Press, 1973), pp. 14-24.

29 While the Saxons, being a minority group themselves, sympathized with the plight of the other minorities in Transylvania, they could not bypass the Jewish question in view of their allegiance to the German fatherland. Fearing that Transylvanian Magyar-Jewish ties would endanger their relations with Nazi Germany, the Saxons sought closer cooperation with Bucharest. The latter had chosen to ally itself with Germany because of differences with the Soviet Union over the Bessarabian question. Saxon fears were confirmed when on April 5, 1926 Hungary signed a "Treaty of Friendship" with Mussolini's Italy in the wake of a growing concern over possible repercussions of German intrusion into Hungary. In March 1934 closer economic and political links were established with Italy and Austria, but Mussolini's preoccupation with Ethiopia in 1935-36 made Hungary uneasy about her heavy reliance on Italy. Events which were beyond her control restricted her choice of alternative solutions. With the Anschluss of March 1938 (German-Austrian union) Germany came drastically close to the Hungarian border, underlining the eminent threat of Nazi occupation. Finally, the Munich Conference of September 1938 established German hegemony over East Central Europe, making concession almost inevitable. As a result of the Austro-German alliance, Magyar-Jewish nationalism in Transylvania took on a distinctly anti-fascist character, losing some of its revisionist flavor. When Count Paul Teleki assumed the premiership in 1939, he suppressed the leading fascist organization, the "Arrow Cross."

30 Gyula Zathureczky, *Transylvania*: *Citadel of the West* (Astor Park: Danubian Press, n.d.), p. 44. Of 5,461,200 acres of land only 1,904,635 acres were owned by farmers possessing over 100 acres. Of this latter estimate, 487,000 belonged to the Rumanian churches and did not fall under land reform. Almost half of the land expropriated from Hungarians was, therefore, taken from those who possessed less than 100 acres.

31 C. A. Macartney, *Hungary and Her Successors*, *op. cit.*, pp. 303-306. As a result of land reform, 119 Catholic parishes were left without any land at all. In 1932 the Magyar Calvinist Church spent 64 million lei annually on its schools, of which the state contributed only 3 million. In 1935 even this subsidy was terminated.

32 Minorities were prohibited from establishing denominational Hungarian-speaking higher schools or training colleges for elementary school teachers. Admission to denominational schools was made dependent on racial origin, judged by religion or an analysis of the surname. The surname in many cases had been romanized and aided in disqualifying candidates. The Rumanian Law of July 1, 1930 introduced a school tax of 14% but this did not supply any allocations to Hungarian schools from the proceeds. It did, however, require these schools to pay the tax. See Tibor Eckhardt's speech to the League of Nations, "Roumanian Treatment of Hungarian Minorities," September 1934. Mr. Eckhardt was the Hungarian representative at the League of Nations.

33 Istvan Csatár, *Erdély és a Visszatért Keleti Részek* (Budapest: Halász Irodalmi és Könyvkiadóvállalat, 1941), pp. 107-108. Written at the time when the Second Vienna Award was still in effect, the English title is: *Transylvania and the Returned Eastern Sections*.

34 See Tibor Eckhardt's speech before the League of Nations, *op. cit.*

35 The 1910 Hungarian census was taken at the end of half a century when Hungary had done everything in her power to promote the knowledge of the Hungarian language. Based on mother tongue or the language spoken best, it does not coincide entirely with the Rumanian criterion used in 1930. Rumania based its census on race. This meant that Jews, for instance, who considered themselves Hungarian by mother tongue were shifted out into the "others" category. Their number came to 6.4% of the urban population in 1930. It is interesting to observe that in hisorical Transylvania which, by the way, was much smaller than the Transylvania of 1930, Hungarians were shown to outnumber Rumanians far more than in 1930. The 1910 census may have favored Hungarians but even amidst the favoritism, the discrepancy between it and the Rumanian figures given for 1930 is immense. For a discussion of Rumanian census data, see Robert R. King, *op. cit.*, pp. 91-92.

36 Istvan Csatár, *op. cit.*, p. 88. The various categories are my translation. For a discussion of the many forms of discrimination against Hungarians, see András Hory, *Még Egy Barázdát Sem* (Munchen: Ledermuller Oliver, 1967).

37 After the famous battle of Mohács in 1526, the Turks devastated a large part of Hungary but then retreated. Pursuant to this decisive date, the Hungarians were able to establish a separate principality in Transylvania which, although paying tribute to the Turks, maintained its independence throughout the 16th and 17th centuries. In a series of campaigns lasting until 1699, the Turks were finally driven out of Hungary. Rumania's independence from Turkey was achieved between 1856 and 1866, a full century and a half after that of Hungary.

38 Gyula Zathureczky, *op. cit.*, p. 49.

39 Robert L. Wolff, *The Balkans in Our Time* (Cambridge: Harvard University Press, 1956), p. 193. Wolff speaks of "long lines of trucks and long freight trains rushing across the new frontier into southern Transylvania..." He also mentions severe persecutions ensuing on both sides.

40 C. L. Sulzberger, "Big Four Quickly Cede All Transylvania to the Rumanians," (*The New York Times*, May 8, 1946), p. 1.

41 C. L. Sulzberger, "Rumania Gets Rule in Transylvania," (*The New York Times*, March 11, 1945), p. 1.

42 *The New York Times*, May 8, 1946. This quote was taken from the article cited above. The administration of Transylvania was actually turned over to Rumania in March 1945. In April 1945, a Hungarian delegation went to Moscow with a proposal to cede 22,000 square kilometers of Transylvania to Hungary. The Soviets were not particularly interested in the Hungarian demands. The Hungarians were, after all, still considered former enemies. Moscow was reticent about making concessions to the Magyars. Molotov suggested that Hungary negotiate directly with Rumania, knowing full well that the latter would decline to do so.

43 Carlton J. H. Hayes, *op. cit.*, p. 5.

44 Note the discussion in the introduction to this paper. Patriotism enters into nationalism, but the doctrine of nationalism is more pragmatic in its essence than the patriotic flavor which accrues to it.

45 V. I. Lenin, "Critical Remarks on the National Question," in *Questions of National Policy and Proletarian Internationalism* (Moscow: Progress Publishers, not dated), p. 30.

46 Elie Kedourie, *op. cit.*, p. 20. Kedourie describes the retrogressive-progressive distinction in very concise and vivid terms.

47 Gyula Zathureczky, *op. cit.*, p. 52.

48 Rezolutii; American Jewish Committee, *The Jews in the Soviet Satellites* (New York, 1953).

49 See also Ghita Ionescu, *Communism in Rumania* 1944-1962 (London: Oxford University Press, 1964), pp. 182-183.

50 For a discussion on rationality in the totalitarian regime see Zbigniew Brzezinski, "Totalitarianism and Rationality," (*The American Political Science Review*, vol. L, September, 1956).

51 Anuarul Statistic al Romaniei, 1937. According to the administrative revisions made in 1945, Crisana, Maramures, and the Bánát constituted three out of the nine provinces in Rumania.

52 See Elie Kedourie's treatment of the linguistic and racial question in *op. cit.*, p. 71.

53 See Fred Pisky, "The People," in Stephen Fischer-Galati, ed., *Romania* (New York: Frederick A. Praeger, 1957), p. 54. Although an urban-rural breakdown is also available, we will not be dealing with that data here. The figures which have been given are advanced as well in Endre Haraszti, *The Ethnic History of Transylvania* (Astor Park: Danubian Press, 1971), p. 169. Since the major segment of the Hungarian population resides in Transylvania, the data reflects their strength in that area closely. The "not declared" category can be attributed to the fact that a number of individuals feared economic, social or political reprisal in declaring their nationality. This fear element may also account for significant shifts into the Rumanian category by some who were actually members of one of the minorities.

54 See the *Statesman's Yearbook* for these figures, 1957 and 1960-61. The data presented in 1960-61 is used in later years as well. I have chosen to limit the comparison to four national groups here since these suffice to illustrate statistical trends.

55 For the 1910 and 1930 figures see Istvan Csatár, *op. cit.*, p. 95. For later data refer to *Statesman's Yearbook*, 1957 and 1967-68.

56 M. Eugene Osterhaven, *Transylvania*: *The Pathos of a Reformation Tradition* (Michigan: The Western Theological Seminary, 1968), p. 12.

57 One must always be wary when looking at Rumanian census figures since their absolute accuracy can be questioned. There may be discrepancies from one source to the next. One also has to be cautious because different criteria are employed from one census to the next, making comparisons a bit difficult.

58 "Population Conditions in Transylvania," *Journal de la Société Hongroise de Statistique* (Budapest, 1939). Also Istvan Csatár, *op. cit.*, p. 95.

59 *Recensamentul General al Populatiei Romane din* 1930, Institutul Central de Statistics, Bucuresti, 1930. Also, see Istvan Csatár, *Ibid.*

60 *Populatis Republicii Populara Romane le* 25 *Januarie* 1948, Institutul Central de Statistics, Bucuresti, 1948. Also see *Statesman's Yearbook*, 1949.

61 *Anuarul Statistic al R.P.R.*, 1960, Bucuresti. A brief look at these trends in Cluj is provided by Osterhaven, *op. cit.*, p. 26. See also *Statesman's Yearbook*, 1957 which gives the total population for 1956 as 154,752.

62 "The Hungarian Minority Problem in Rumania," *Bulletin of the International Commission of Jurists*, No. 17 in Gallus, Alexander, ed., *Studies for a New Central Europe* (New York: Mid-European Research Institute, 1964).

63 C. L. Sulzberger, "Rumania Gets Rule in Transylvania" (*The New York Times*, March 11, 1945), p. 1.

64 Ghita Ionescu, *op. cit.*, p. 195.

65 International Court of Justice, *Interpretation of Peace Treaties with Bulgaria, Hungary, and Rumania; Pleadings*, & *c.*: Advisory Opinions of March 30th and July 18th 1950, p. 28.

66 Constitution of the People's Republic of Rumania (September 24, 1952), Articles 17, 19, 20, 21, 81, 82, 84.

67 Robert R. King, *op. cit.*, *pp.* 150, 156.

70

68 In 1950 there were still 28 regions. The 1952 Constitution reduced the number of regions to 18, including the Magyar Autonomous Region. Approximately one-third of the Hungarian population of Rumania came under its jurisdiction. Based on an organic state model in which the territorial principle involved granting autonomy to certain administrative areas, the territory in question did not include the predominantly Magyar region of Cluj (257,974 Hungarians) or Brasov (108,751 Hungarians)—figures are given according to the 1956 census. The Rumanian government obviously sought to keep the Magyar area as small as possible.

69 Robert R. King, op. cit., pp. 150-152. Since the Autonomous Region had a Hungarian majority, it was able to adhere to the constitutional provision for choosing civil servants from the majority. As late as 1958, Scinteia asserts, 78% of the civil servants were members of national minorities, principally Hungarian, along with 80% of the deputies to the People's Council. See Scinteia, July 24, 1958.

70 Gheorghiu-Dej, as the First Secretary of the Rumanian Worker's Party, was much more powerful than Chivu Stoica, the Premier and President of the Council of Ministers.

71 The notion of a Kossuth type of Danubian federation was discussed earlier in this paper. It was raised as an issue during the uprising of 1956. On October 26, 1956, the student parliament of Miskolc was demanding federation while on November 1, 1956, Magyar Szabadság cited its establishment as "the most specific demand of our national foreign policy." Imre Nagy favored some sort of cooperative union as well. See Robert R. King, op. cit., p. 78.

72 Kedourie raised this idea, op. cit., p. 117 and I have tried to confirm its relevance here.

73 Welles Hangen, "Rumania Arrests Unruly Magyars," (The New York Times, October 30, 1956), p. 17.

74 Welles Hangen, "Rumania Appeals to Her Minorities," (The New York Times, October 29, 1956), p. 9.

75 Welles Hangen, "Rumania Backs Soviet on Rebels," (The New York Times, November 3, 1956), p. 12.

76 "U.S. and Rumania Break Off Talks," (The New York Times, November 4, 1956), p. 34.

77 "Demonstrations Reported," (*The New York Times*, November 1, 1956), p. 24.

78 Welles Hangen, "Rumania Forbids Visits to Four Areas," (*The New York Times*, November 1, 1956), p. 1.

79 Welles Hangen, "Rumania Backs Soviet on Rebels," (*The New York Times*, November 3, 1956), p. 12.

80 Radio Bucharest, February 27, 1958. See also Robert R. King, *op. cit.*, p. 89.

81 *Pravda*, November 26, 1956. See also *Ibid.*, p. 84

82 "Ethnic and Political Persecution in Rumania," *The Congressional Record*, August 8, 1964.

83 *Ibid.*

84 Edward Crankshaw, "Hungarian Minority Fears Rumanian Axe," (*The New York Herald Tribune*, April 15, 1963).

85 George Bailey, "Trouble Over Transylvania," (*The Reporter*, November 19, 1964).

86 Gyula Zathureczky, *op. cit.*, pp. 55-56.

87 Robert R. King, *op. cit.*, p. 153.

88 George Bailey, "Trouble Over Transylvania," (*The Reporter*, November 19, 1964).

89 *Statesman's Yearbook*, 1952, 1953, 1954, 1958, 1962-63.

90 *Der Spiegel*, No. 45 (October 31, 1966), pp. 158-162. The German paper reported several incidents of suicide. One incident was mentioned by George A. Hay, "National Minority Problems" in Kurt London, ed., *Eastern Europe in Transition*, (Baltimore: The Johns Hopkins Press, 1966), p. 133. Hay refers to the pro-rector, László Szabadi, his wife and five other university professors who committed suicide.

91 Robert R. King, *op. cit.*, pp. 153-154. See also *Scinteia*, February 22, 1959. For details of the final merger see *Scinteia*, July 3, 1959 and *The New York Times*, June 10, 1959.

92 Michel Tatu, *Le Monde*, November 11, 1967. See also Robert R. King, *op. cit.*, p. 154; also, M. Eugene Osterhaven, *op. cit.*, p. 39; also, *Scinteia*, July 3, 1959.

93 Robert M. MacKisson, "Letter to the American Transylvanian Federation," June 4, 1963; also, refer to *The Congressional Record*, Mr. Lindsay's speech on "Communist Mistreatment of Hungarians in Transylvania," July 22, 1964.

94 *The Congressional Record*, August 8, 1964.

95 The two districts detached from the Magyar Autonomous Region were Sfintu Gheorghe (85.3% Hungarian) and Tirgu Secuiesc (90.2% Hungarian). The three districts added so as to form the Mures-Magyar Autonomous Region were Ludus (22.1% Hungarian); Sarmas (13.7% Hungarian); and Tirnaveni (25.6% Hungarian). Rumanians in the new Region increased their ranks from 146,830 (20%) to 266,403 (35%). Hungarians decreased their ranks from 565,510 (77%) to 473,154 (62%). See Robert R. King, *op. cit.*, pp. 156-157.

96 *Le Monde*, July 4, 1964.

97 Gyula Zathureczky, "National Minorities, Step-Children in Communist Lands," in Gallus, Alexander, ed., *Studies for a New Central Europe*, op. cit., vol. 1, No. 2, p. 37.

98 *The Congressional Record*, August 8, 1964.

99 Edward Crankshaw, *op. cit.*

100 *Neue Zuricher Zeitung*, December 3, 1967.

101 Covasna County was formed from the two Székely districts of Sfintu Gheorghe and Tirgu Secuiesc. It was the smallest county in Rumania. Harghita ranked fifth from the bottom. Their combined population according to the 1966 census was no more than 459,250. See Robert R. King, *op. cit.*, pp. 161-162.

102 See the trends depicted in the *Statesman's Yearbook*, 1960-1968.

103 The entire text of this statement appeared in *Népszabadság*, July 2, 1966.

104 *Scinteia*, July 12, 1971.

105 *Magyar Hirlap*, August 4, 1971.

106 Radio Moscow in Rumanian, July 6, 1971.

107 *Sovietskaya Rossiya*, August 8, 1971.

108 Radio Moscow in Rumanian, August 8, 1971. Also note that reference is made to these Soviet-Rumanian debates in Robert R. King, *op. cit.*, pp. 167-168.

BIBLIOGRAPHY

Andics, Erzsébet, *A Magyar Nacionalizmus Kialakulása és Története*, (Budapest: Kossuth, 1964).

Bratianu, G. I., *Rumanien und Ungarn: Demographische und Wirtschaftliche Betrachtungen* (Bucharest: Institutul de Stunte Morale si Politice, 1940).

Central Statistical Board, Statistical Pocket Book of the Socialist Republic of Romania, 1966, 1967, 1969.

Cornish, Louis C., *Transylvania: The Land Beyond the Forest*, (Philadelphia: Dorrance & Company, Inc., 1947).

Csatár, István, *Erdély és a Visszatért Keleti Részek*, (Budapest: Halász Irodalmi és Könyvkiadóvállalat, 1941).

Déer, József and László Gáldi, *Magyarok és Románok* (Budapest: Athenaeum Irodalmi és Nyomdai Részvénytársulat Nyomása, 1941).

Fischer-Galati, Stephen, *The New Rumania*, (M.I.T. Press, 1967).

Fischer-Galati, Stephen, ed., *Romania* (New York: Frederick A. Praeger, 1957).

Fischer-Galati, Stephen, ed., *Eastern Europe in the Sixties* (New York: Frederick A. Praeger, 1963).

Floyd, David, *Rumania: Russia's Dissident Ally*, (New York: Frederick A. Praeger, 1965).

Gallus, Alexander, ed., *Studies for a New Central Europe*, (New York: The Mid-European Research Institute, 1964).

Haraszti, Endre, *The Ethnic History of Transylvania*, (Astor Park: The Danubian Press, 1971).

Hayes, Carlton J. H., *Essays on Nationalism*, (New York: The MacMillan Co., 1926).

Hayes, Carlton J. H., *The Historical Evolution of Modern Nationalism*, (New York: The MacMillan Co., 1949).

Hory, András, *Még Egy Barázdát Sem* (München: Ledermüller Oliver, 1967).

Ionescu, Ghita, *Communism in Rumania, 1944-1962*, (London: Oxford University Press, 1964).

Iorga, Nicolae, *A History of Rumania*, (New York: Ams Press, 1970).

Kádár, János, *Hazafiság és Internacionalizmus*, (Budapest: Kossuth, 1968).

Kedourie, Elie, *Nationalism*, (New York: Frederick A. Praeger, 1960).

75

King, Robert R., *Minorities Under Communism*, (Cambridge: Harvard University Press, 1973).

Kohn, Hans, *The Idea of Nationalism*, (New York: The MacMillan Co., 1961).

Kormos, C., *Rumania* (Cambridge: University Press, 1944).

Lenin, V. I., *Questions of National Policy and Proletarian Internationalism*, (Moscow: Progress Publishers, n.d.).

Lichtheim, George, *Marxism: An Historical and Critical Study*, (New York: Praeger Publishers, 1973).

London, Kurt ed., *Eastern Europe in Transition*, (Baltimore: The Johns Hopkins Press, 1966).

Macartney, C. A., *Hungary: A Short History*, (Chicago: Aldine Publishing Co., 1949).

Macartney, C. A., *Problems of the Danube Basin*, (Cambridge: University Press, 1942).

Macartney, C. A., *National States and National Minorities* (London: Oxford University Press, 1934).

Macartney, C. A., *Hungary and Her Successors, 1919-1937*, (London: Oxford University Press, 1965).

Macartney, C. A., *October Fifteenth, A History of Modern Hungary, 1929-1945 Parts I and II*, (Edinburgh: At the University Press, 1961).

Magyar Történelmi Társulat, ed., *Erdély* (Budapest: Athenaeum Irodalmi és Nyomdai Részvénytársulat Nyomása, 1940).

Makkai, László, *Magyar-Román Közös Mult*, (Budapest: Teleki Pál Tudományos Intézet, 1948).

Manuila, Sabin, *Aspects Démographiques de la Transylvanie*, (Bucharest: L'Institut Central de Statistique, 1938).

Meyer, Alfred G., *Leninism*, (New York: Frederick A. Praeger, 1972).

Molnár, József & Borbándi, Gyula, ed. *Tanulmányok a Magyar Forradalomról* (Munchen: Aurora Könyvek, 1966).

Montgomery, John Flournoy, *Hungary: The Unwilling Satellite*, (New York: The Devin-Adair Company, 1947).

Nyirő, József, *Mi Az Igazság Erdély Esetében?* (Cleveland: Katolikus Magyar Vasárnapja, n.d.).

Osterhaven, M. Eugene, *Transylvania: The Pathos of a Reformation Tradition*, A Reformed Review Occasional Paper (Michigan: The Western Theological Seminary, 1968).

Robinson, William F., *Nationalism: Hungarian Problem Child*. (Munich: Radio Free Europe Research, July 5, 1967).

Roucek, Joseph S. *Contemporary Roumania and Her Problems: A Study in Modern Nationalism* (Stanford: Stanford University Press, 1932).

Seton-Watson, Hugh, *The East European Revolution*, 2nd Edition (New York: Frederick A. Praeger, 1951).

Seton-Watson, Hugh, *Eastern Europe Between the Wars*, 1918-1941, (New York: Harper and Row, 1967).

Seton-Watson, R. W., *Transylvania: A Key Problem*, (Oxford: The Classic Press, 1943).

Seton-Watson, R. W., *A History of the Roumanians*, (Connecticut: Archon Books, 1962).

Sinanian, Sylvia, István Deák and Peter Ludz, ed., *Eastern Europe in the 1970's*, (New York: Praeger Publishers, 1972).

Sugar, Peter F., and Ivo J. Lederer, *Nationalism in Eastern Europe*, (Seattle and London: University of Washington Press, 1969).

Szász, Zsombor De, *The Minorities in Roumanian Transylvania*, (London: The Richards Press, 1927).

Szekfü, Gyula, *Allam és Nemzet*, (Budapest: Magyar Szemle Társaság, 1942).

Teleki, Pál, *The Evolution of Hungary and Its Place in European History*, (New York: The MacMillan Co., 1923).

Toma, Peter A., ed., *The Changing Face of Communism in Eastern Europe*, (Arizona: The University of Arizona Press, 1970).

Transylvanus, *The Ethnical Minorities of Transylvania*, (London: Eyre and Spottiswoode Ltd., 1934).

Wickersham, George W., *Opinion: Regarding the Rights of Hungarian and of Certain Hungarian Nationals Under the Treaty of Tianon* (New York, 1928).

Wolff, Robert Lee, *The Balkans in Our Time*, (Cambridge: Harvard University Press, 1956).

Zathureczky, Gyula, *Transylvania: Citadel of the West*, (Astor Park: The Danubian Press, n.d.).

ARTICLES AND PERIODICALS

The American Political Science Review

The Congressional Record

The Hungarian Quarterly

Irodalmi Ujság (Paris)

Magyar Elet (Toronto)

Magyar Hirlap

Le Monde

Népszabadság

Neue Zuricher Zeitung

The New York Herald Tribune

The New York Times

Pravda

The Reporter

Scinteia

Sovietskaya Rossiya

Der Spiegel

The Statesman's Yearbook

Világhiradó (Cleveland)

APPENDIX

I. AN HISTORICAL BACKGROUND

The Hungarian minority in Rumania is concentrated mostly in the historical province of Transylvania separated from the rest of Rumania by a continuous mountain chain (Carpathian Mountains) ranging between 3000-7500 feet. There are also Hungarians in Bucharest (estimates range as high as 100,000) and in western Moldavia.

Transylvania, along with the other districts of the Bánát and eastern Hungary attached to Rumania in 1920, was a part of the Kingdom of Hungary between 1001 A.D. and 1919.

Transylvania, under the name of Dacia, was a province of the Roman Empire between 109 and 271 A.D. Upon their departure, the Romans evacuated the population of the province and destroyed its cities. The population was resettled in Moesia which is today northern Bulgaria. Following the collapse of Roman rule, numerous migrating tribes invaded the region. They were of Germanic, Hunno-Avaric and Slavonic origin. Hungarians started settling in Transylvania in the tenth century.

Hungarian kings tried to draw German settlers to the region between 1161-1200. The German settlers were known as Saxons. The Saxons retained their local administrative autonomy.

There is no historical record of the Rumanian presence in Transylvania prior to 1210 A.D., except for the chronicles of Simon Kézai and Magister P (osa), better known as "Anonymus." Rumanian historians generally accept the Daco-Roman theory of continuous Rumanian settlement of Transylvania between 271 A.D. and 1210 A.D. Their best argument remains the undoubtedly Roman origin of the Rumanian language. They gloss over the historical silence of almost a millennium and point out that the Roman settlers who stayed behind could have survived in the mountainous areas without their presence being recorded in historical documents.

Etymological research even by Rumanian scholars like Capidan, however, seems to prove that the Rumanian language originated in Italy, was developed in southern Albania and moved to the north. There are isolated groups today in Yugoslavia which still speak dialects closely akin to Rumanian. If we add the silence of historical sources to these etymological findings, the Daco-Roman theory remains a hypothesis at best.

On the other hand, there is nothing hypothetical about the presence of Hungarians in Transylvania since as far back as the tenth century. After 1001 A.D., Transylvania formed an integral part of the Hungarian Kingdom founded by St. Stephen. It was administered by the oldest son of the king, the Hungarian equivalent of the Prince of Wales.

Following the capture of the Hungarian capital by the Turks in 1541, Transylvania became a semi-independent principality paying tribute to the Sultan but not occupied by the Turks. Its princes were all Hungarians. Most of the princes were Protestants, except for the Bathorys. Stephen Bathory, in turn, also became the King of Poland and spread the fame of Transylvania to all of Europe.

The cultural accomplishments of Transylvanians in the 17th century were very high and constituted the mainstream of Hungarian culture in arts and sciences. It was during this period that the first Rumanian books appeared, mostly bibles and religious literature subsidized by the Hungarian princes. In the 18th century, Transylvania was the home of the greatest mathematician of his time, John Bolyai, and of the renowned Orientalist, Alexander Korossy-Csoma, both Hungarians.

Upon the capture of Buda by the forces of the Emperor-King, and the subsequent death of Prince Michael Apaffy, Transylvania was administered by the Habsburg King as a separate province known as the "Grand Principality of Transylvania". Legally it remained a part of the Kingdom of the Crown of St. Stephen.

The Turkish raids in the 17th century decimated the Hungarian and German populations of the Central Plains (Mezőség) and the river valleys. The Rumanians, mostly mountaineers, suffered least from the invasions. Yet, by the end of the century, Rumanians were still inferior in numbers to Hungarians.

During the period between 1691-1780, the governors of Transylvania were mostly Hungarians except for the Saxon, Baron von Bruckenthal. They were anxious to repopulate the province. With Turkish rule continuing in the Rumanian provinces of Moldavia and Wallachia, Rumanian settlers were readily available and by 1760, Rumanians had become a significant national force in Transylvania.

The ideas of the French Revolution permeated the Austrian Empire, despite the balancing acts of Prince Metternich. Nationalism became popular at first in Hungary and Croatia, then among Transylvanian Rumanians. The "reform age" of 1825-48 produced outstanding leaders among Transylvanian Hungarians, including Count Nicholas Wesselényi and the writer-politician, Baron Nicholas Josika.

When the events of March 1848 resulted in Habsburg concessions to Hungary, including the formation of a government responsible to the Parliament, the reintegration of Transylvania into Hungary was also accomplished.

By 1848 the Rumanians were already well-organized through the Rumanian Orthodox Church. They opposed any union with Hungary. Encouraged by the Vienna Court, they revolted under the leadership of Avram Iancu and Archbishop Saguna. Guerrilla fighting continued for almost a year. Temporarily at least, the Hungarians won and the Rumanians made peace with them on the basis of local autonomy. A few weeks later, however,

Russian troops entered Hungary as allies of the Emperor-King and crushed the Hungarian armies.

For seventeen years the Austrians governed Transylvania, oppressing both Hungarians and Rumanians, bringing the two nationalities closer to one another. When the Austro-Hungarian Compromise was arranged in 1867 and Transylvania was constitutionally reunited with Hungary, there were no Rumanian protests.

Hungary enacted a liberal Nationalities Law in 1868 giving equal rights to all its citizens, including the right to education in the mother tongue. As a result, by 1914 there were about 2,400 Rumanian private schools, 12 high schools and several Rumanian language colleges in Hungary.

Rumanian deputies were elected from predominantly Rumanian districts to the Budapest Parliament. Economic affluence and cultural development characterized the period between 1867-1914. A strong Rumanian middle class arose and economic self-help organizations assisted Rumanian farmers in buying land.

Yet, alienation between the educated Hungarian and Rumanian classes continued to grow. Cultural reliance on the "Old Kingdom" of Rumania aroused the concern of the Hungarian Government. Nevertheless, when war broke out in 1914, the Hungarian and Rumanian regiments fought equally well and there was no changing of sides by Rumanian units. Rumania herself declared neutrality, although on paper, she was still an ally of the Central Powers. But by the summer of 1916 she had joined the Allies. The Treaty of London promised her Transylvania, the Bánát and some districts of eastern Hungary. Rumanian troops proceeded to enter Transylvania, only to be defeated by the German and Austrian-Hungarian armies. In March 1918 Rumania concluded a peace treaty with Germany and Austria-Hungary, but on November 7, 1918 she declared war on the Austro-Hungarian monarchy which had signed an armistice with the Allies on November 2, 1918. Assisted by the Allied High Command in Belgrade and by a Hungarian Government anxious to avoid a conflict, the Rumanian army steadily advanced into Transylvania without meeting resistance. Encouraged by Allied support, the Rumanian National Party in Hungary claimed already in October 1918 before the collapse of the Monarchy the sole right to represent the Rumanians of Hungary. When the Hungarian National Council assumed power on October 30, 1918, a Rumanian National Council was also established to oversee the Rumanian-inhabited regions of Transylvania and eastern Hungary.

The new Hungarian government offered an honorable solution at the negotiating table at Arad in November 1918. Minister Jaszi recognized the Rumanian people's right to decide its own future in accordance with the Wilsonian principles. Rumanian-inhabited territories would be administered by the Rumanian National Council on a cantonal basis and a government would be created which would cooperate with the Hungarian National Government on "matters of common interest." In this way, all past demands of Rumanians in Hungary would be satisfied and a Hungarian-Transylvanian

Confederation would be created. The Rumanian National Council, reassured of Allied support for a union with Rumania, turned down the Hungarian offer. However, even the Rumanian Council paid lip service to the Wilsonian principles by stating that the Rumanian nation "undertook the obligation to the Wilsonian principles where the other peoples on these territories were concerned and was ready to guarantee each people the conditions required for its free national development." (*Unification of the Romanian National State, Bucharest: Academy of the Socialist Republic of Rumania*, 1972, p. 245).

On December 1, 1918, the Rumanian Transylvanians convened at Alba Julia (Gyulafehérvár) and after bitter debate, voted for union with the Kingdom of Rumania. Yet, the delegates to the convention were not elected by universal ballot. 628 of the 1,000 delegates were appointed by church, militia, and civic associations and parties. (*Unification of the Romanian National State, op. cit.*, p. 244). The declaration of December 1, 1918 still promised:

> Full national liberty for all coinhabiting peoples. Each people shall assemble, administer, and render justice in its maternal tongue by persons coming from its midst, and each people shall be given the right of representation in the legislative bodies and the government of the country, in proportion to the number of its members.
> Equal rights and full religious liberty for all denominations in the state.

(*Unification of the Romanian National State, op. cit.*, p. 283).

At the meeting, the argument which swayed the majority toward a union with Rumania was the assurance by Rumanian leaders that the Peace Conference would allot Transylvania to Rumania.

In the Peace Treaty of Trianon (1920), Rumania received nearly the same territories as were promised to her in the Treaty of London. The Allied Powers insisted, in turn, upon the compliance of Rumania with the Minorities Treaty. The provisions of this treaty were never fully kept, but its existence prevented a more intense persecution of Hungarians. As a result of the Peace Treaty, 180,000 Hungarians left Transylvania (former civil servants). The remainder became second-class citizens in the Rumanian state.

Interestingly enough, the Transylvanian Rumanians were also disappointed as their compatriots from the "old Kingdom" took over the reins of state power. Although unfriendly toward the Hungarians, the Transylvanian Rumanian leaders, many of them former deputies of the Hungarian Parliament, became the most severe critics of the new regime. Political and financial corruption flourished and extremist movements, like the rightist Iron Guard, threatened the Hungarian minority.

The land reform confiscated mostly Hungarian estates, as their Rumanian counterparts were exempted due to various legal loopholes. Literary language requirements, in turn, prevented equal representation of Hungarians in the civil service. A certain percentage of workers and employees in every business enterprise in Rumania had to be ethnic Rumanians. Hungarian students had only a remote chance of passing Rumanian admission tests for the universities. Many Hungarian church schools were forced to be closed and Rumanians were settled into the purely Hungarian counties of southeastern Transylvania. The arising disputes led to innumerable protests to the League of Nations and despite the generally friendly attitude toward Rumania by most League members, the Rumanians were adjudicated against many times by the League and the Hague Court of International Justice.

Hungarian culture, however, continued to flourish even under Rumanian censorship. Many of the best known Hungarian writers and poets of the century belonged to the "Transylvanian" school of the interwar period like Aron Tamási, Joseph Nyirő, Albert Wass, Alexander Reményik and Charles Kos.

A Western ally in 1939, Rumania was put in an untenable position in June 1940 upon the collapse of France. Hungary began pressing for a frontier revision. The U.S.S.R., with German assent under the 1939 Pact, demanded the return of Bessarabia and northern Bukovina. Rumania yielded to the Soviet ultimatum but came to no agreement wih Hungary. Anxious to assure the acquisition of the oil producing region of Ploesti for Germany, Hitler intervened. Germany and Italy decided upon the Vienna Award on August 30, 1940 partitioning Transylvania between Hungary and Rumania. Most of the Hungarian-inhabited areas and some Rumanian areas were returned to Hungary while some Hungarian districts still remained with Rumania. A clear-cut nationality division was impossible in the case of Transylvania.

Although Rumania entered World War II on the German side, she was successfully invaded by the Soviets. In August 1944, she switched camps. The war ended with Rumania on the side of the victorious Soviet army. The armistice of August 23, 1944 gave her the administration of northern Transylvania. Yet, the atrocities committed by returning Rumanian units were such that the Red Army had to expel the Rumanian administration and establish its own in October 1944. This has been the only known instance of the Red Army directly intervening to save Transylvania's inhabitants against local terrorists. Only after Gromyko's visit to Bucharest following the Yalta Conference which resulted in the establishment of a Communist-dominated coalition government in Bucharest did the U.S.S.R. agree to return the northern part of Transylvania to Rumanian administration. At the Paris Peace Conference of 1946, the United States favored the return of the Hungarian-inhabited frontier zone to Hungary.

Because of Soviet pressure, the new Rumanian coalition government, dominated by the Communist Party, promised a fair solution to the Hungarian question in Transylvania. Originally, all Hungarian-inhabited regions were to receive an autonomous status but even after the promulgation of the 1952 Constitution, only the southeastern Hungarian counties received their autonomy, and the unit was diluted by the addition of several Rumanian districts to the main body.

The 1952 Constitution guaranteed no discrimination on the basis of national origin, use of the mother tongue in courts and before all public authorities and also the right of parents to send their children to the schools of their choice. All chauvinist propaganda was barred, a measure unfortunately usually enforced against protesting Hungarians.

Religious persecution was severe during this period. The worst fate befell the Greek Uniate Church to which about one-third of the Transylvanian Rumanians and close to 200,000 Hungarians also belonged. In 1948 a governmental decree merged it with the Rumanian Orthodox Church. Its bishops either had to accept the merger, or like Bishop Julius Hossu, were jailed. Its clergy experienced a similar fortune and many died in prison. The Roman Catholic Church also suffered. Hundreds of priests and the Bishop of Alba Julia (Gyulafehérvár) were jailed for varying periods of time.

II. GEOPOLITICAL AND DEMOGRAPHIC FEATURES
OF TRANSYLVANIA.

Geographically, Transylvania forms a plateau surrounded by high mountains in the east, south and north. The only sizeable opening lies in the northwest where the province opens toward the Hungarian Plains. There is also a natural opening through the Maros (Mures) valley leading to the Hungarian Plains. Passes toward Wallachia are few and there are only three routes toward Bucharest and Craiova. The situation is similar toward Moldavia in the east.

Thus, geographically and historically Transylvania is connected with the Hungarian Plains rather than with the Rumanian provinces of Wallachia and Moldavia.

Demographically, Transylvania consists of two major groups: Rumanians and Hungarians. The number of Germans was reduced by their flight in 1944 and subsequent deportations to about 400,000. In the Bánát there are also some Serbs. About 40,000 of the 75,000 Jews remaining in Rumania reside in Transylvania.

The number and percentage of the Hungarian minority is difficult to determine exactly. Rumananian statistics consistently underreport their number. According to these statistics, there was a decrease in the number of Hungarians between 1910-1956 and only a very slight increase between 1956-66. Their number now is about the same as it was in 1910, 161 million. At the same time, the Hungarian-language publication in Rumania, *Korunk,* reported in November 1957 that the natural increase in the Autonomous Hungarian Region was 1.27 percent in 1957 alone.

Many authors, therefore, doubt the accuracy of the Rumanian statistics. A Rumanian author, living in the West, G. Satmarescu, writing in January 1975 in *East Central Europe,* edited by Professor Fischer-Galati of the University of Colorado, estimated the number of unreported and assimilated Hungarians in Transylvania to 900,000, arriving at a final figure of 2.5 million. The *Handbuch Europaischer Volksgruppen* (Reference Book on European Nationality Groups) published in 1974 by the European Union movement, estimated the number of Hungarians in Rumania to be 2.4 million. The Brazilian Transylvanian organization, *Movimento pro Transilvania,* using demographic constants of the overall population increase in Rumania and subtracting changes extraneous to the natural increase arrived at an estimate of 2.816,555 million. Whatever the true figure, it is substantially higher than that of the Rumanian statistical sources and is probably closer to the figures cited by Satmarescu and the editors of the Reference Book on European Nationalities.

Transylvanian Hungarians are thus placed into the position of being the largest national minority in Europe. The continuous abridgment of their human rights and fundamental freedoms assumes more than local importance.

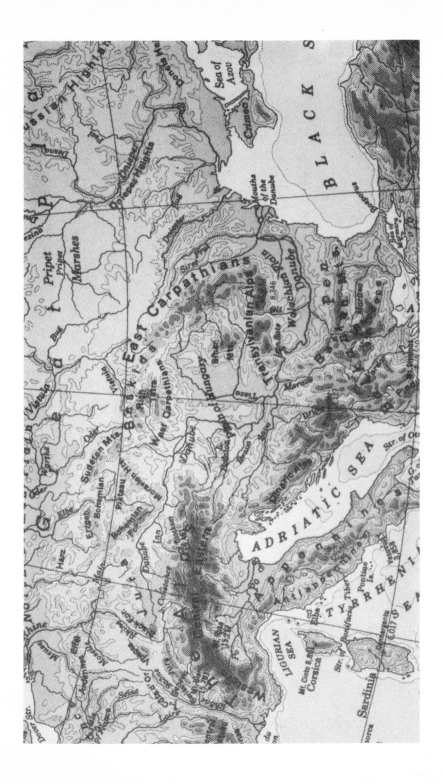

ROBERT RAY KING